THE HANDS-ON SURVIVAL MANUAL FOR MUSICIANS

Bobby Owsinski

Alfred Music Publishing Co., Inc.
P.O. Box 10003
Van Nuys, CA 91410-0003
alfred.com

ISBN-10: 0-7390-8600-6 (Book & DVD)
ISBN-13: 978-0-7390-8600-1 (Book & DVD)

Cover Photos
Microphone: © Dreamstime.com / Gavin Dunt • Camouflage: © iStockphoto.com / Patrick Wong • Equipment: © Bobby Owsinski

 **Alfred Cares.** Contents printed on 100% recycled paper.

CONTENTS

CHAPTER 3

BASIC RECORDING GEAR
.... 23

CHAPTER 4
RECORDING BASICS 35

CHAPTER 5
MICROPHONE PLACEMENT BASICS 43

CHAPTER 6

RECORDING THE DRUMS 51

CHAPTER 7

RECORDING GUITAR AND BASS 71

CHAPTER 8

VOCAL MIKING TECHNIQUES

CHAPTER 9

RECORDING ACOUSTIC INSTRUMENTS

CHAPTER 10

RECORDING ELECTRONIC INSTRUMENTS

CHAPTER 11

RECORDING IN STEREO

CHAPTER 14

PREFACE

WELCOME TO THE AUDIO RECORDING BASIC TRAINING. NOW, LISTEN UP, RECRUITS!

You're probably reading this book for one of many reasons. Maybe you're new to recording and you're not entirely sure if you're doing it right or not. Maybe the sounds you've been recording are wimpy and small and you don't know why. Or maybe you feel like you know the basics but want to learn how the pros do it. That's where I come in, your recording basic training drill instructor.

Like all basic training, this one is intense and makes you work. It's built totally around exercises where you learn recording by actually doing it yourself, and I'm going to guide you every step of the way.

Recording is one of those things that you can't learn by reading—you have to exercise your eyes and ears, and the more you do it, the better you become at it. The problem is that many engineers just starting out don't know where to begin, and those that already know a little don't know what to do to get better.

As your recording drill instructor, I'll take you through all the areas of recording that will not only get you going on the right track, but possibly cut a lot of time off your learning curve. Rather than just covering the theory of recording, you'll be choosing and placing microphones so that you'll learn the secrets of recording faster and easier than you ever thought possible. Along the way I'll tell you the reasons behind the exercises as well as the specifics of what you're learning, but almost every topic in the book is strictly hands-on.

You still have to put in the work, but if you're into making your music sound better, you'll have a lot of fun along the way.

Hopefully you'll find the exercises enjoyable and each one to be a great learning experience. Sometimes an exercise may seem a bit off the wall at first because it may be showing why not to do something, but it will be followed up with another that will show you some major league technique that you can use every time you record.

My goal is to teach you all the things that make a recording sound great, and everything you can do to make it sound bad as well. You may find you'll learn more from the latter than the former.

Please note that I've included a number of examples on the DVD that you can learn from and play with, but feel free to use your own tracks if you have them.

Also note that this book won't cover basic theory of signal flow of a mixing console or DAW. Refer to your instruction manual, or a book like *The Recording Engineer's Handbook* for more insight into this area. If fact, *The Recording Engineer's Handbook* is also a great place to continue learning after you've finished this book, as it will give you a number of additional techniques that you can experiment with.

Okay, recruit. Now hit the deck and give me 20, as we dig deep into the world of recording.

CHAPTER 1
MONITORING

Okay, listen up, recruits! It's time to get your barracks in order.

You can't tell if what you're recording is any good if you can't hear it properly, that's why it's important to have your monitoring system set up correctly during recording.

You can have the best monitoring chain that money can buy, but if it isn't set up correctly in your room, your recordings are going to be disappointing. On the other hand, even if you have inexpensive monitor speakers, you can get surprisingly good results if they're placed correctly in the room. That's why you have to tighten up your listening environment before you begin to record.

The Listening Environment

Let's face it. Unless you're purpose-building your studio from the ground up, it's easy to overlook your listening environment. Usually it's just the old "throw some speakers and a DAW in an open corner of the room and go" routine and leave it at that. While it's possible that you can get lucky with a balanced frequency response and wide stereo field by just setting up a couple of nearfield monitors in your room without thinking much about it, usually that's not the case because normal garages, living rooms, and bedrooms aren't intended as listening spaces and have little in the way of acoustic treatment. Whether you're treating your room or not (you really should—read my book *The Studio Builder's Handbook* for inexpensive ways to do it), the following steps are necessary to optimize what you're hearing.

The correct placement of the speakers is one of the most critical adjustments that you can make in improving the sound of your room. Before you do anything else, this place must be determined. Sometimes, even just a movement of a few inches backwards or forwards can make a big difference.

Determining The Listening Position

The first thing to do is to select the best place in the room for your listening position. The place that provides the best acoustic performance will almost always come from setting up lengthwise in the room because it's easier to avoid some of the room reflections (see Figure 1.1) that can plague the frequency response of the room. In other words, the speakers should be firing the long way down the room.

Standing Waves

Without getting too technical, every room suffers from reflections that reinforce at the 50% point of the room, and diminish at the 25% and 75% points. That means that if your listening position is exactly half-way in the room, one of the low frequencies (which one depends upon the size of the room) will be extremely loud, but that same frequency might be non-existent at the 25% and 75% of the length of the room. This is called a "standing wave."

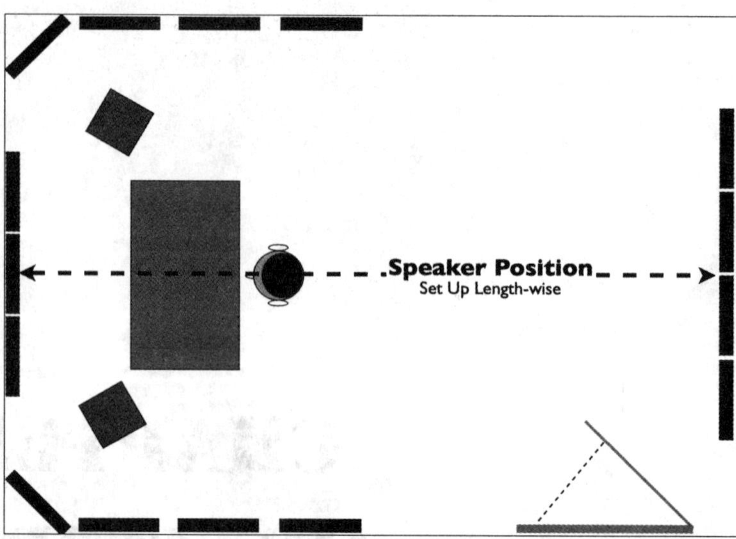

Figure 1.1 - Speaker Placement In The Long Part Of The Room

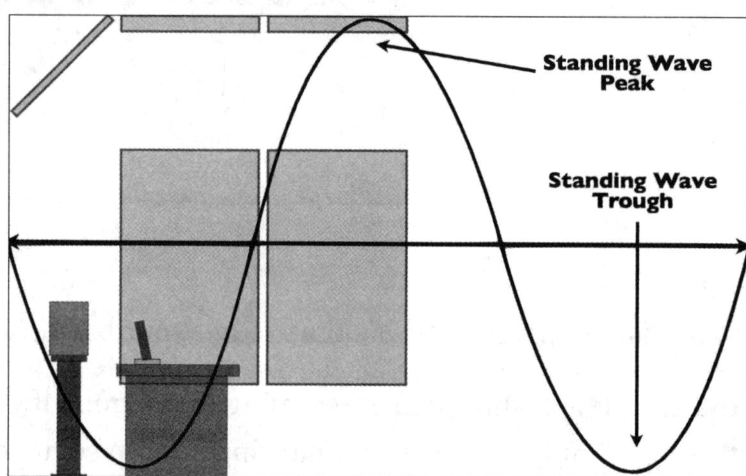

Figure 1.2: A Typical Standing Wave

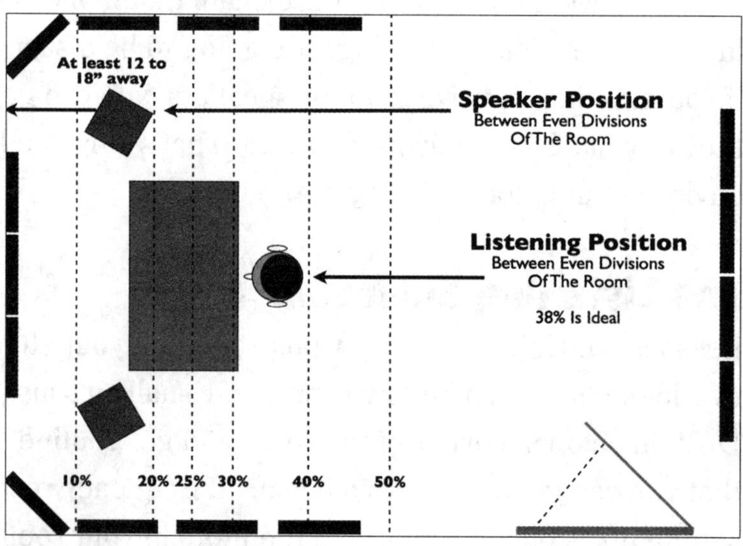

Figure 1.3: Placement In The Room

For example, in a typical room with a 12-foot length, the standing wave will be 47Hz (determined by the formula 1,130 ft. per sec. [the speed of sound]/12 feet x 2), which means that frequency will evenly bounce back and forth in the room. If you place either the speaker or the listening position mid-way in the room, which means at the 50% point, 47Hz will reinforce and it will sound extremely loud. If you place the speakers or listening position at either a quarter of the way into the room (at the 25% point) or a quarter of the way from the rear wall (at the 75% point), 47Hz will cancel out (see Figure 1.2).

As a result, you want to place both the speakers and listening position somewhere in between the 25, 50, and 75 percent points of the room (30, 40, 60, and 80 percent are good to stay away from as well), and place the speakers and listening area at an odd non-divisible number like 27, 38, 45, etc. percent (see Figure 1.3). Although these placement points will get you in the ballpark, prepare to move everything a few inches forward or backwards even after you've placed everything.

There are so many variables involved with just about any room that even the best designers with the best acoustic test gear can't even precisely predict the correct placement, and as a result, may spend an entire week just tweaking the speaker and listening placement, so don't be surprised if it takes some time and experimentation to get this right.

While these numbers may be all well and good, they don't help you much if you don't have that much space to play with. If that's the case, the following quick fixes can still make a considerable difference.

Acoustic Quick Fixes

Without having to acoustically treat your room (which should always come first if you can), here are a few simple things that you can do to instantly improve the performance of your playback system.

- **Avoid placing the speakers up against a wall.** This usually results in some strong peaks in the low frequency response. The further away you can get from the wall, the less it influences the frequency response of your monitors and the smoother that response will be. Figure an absolute minimum of 12 inches, although more is better, as long as you stay out of the 25% point of the room as mentioned earlier.

- **Avoid the corners of the room.** Even more severe than the wall is a corner, since it will reinforce the low end even more than when placed against a wall. The worst is if only one speaker is in the corner, which causes the response of your system to be lopsided on the low-end towards the speaker located there.

- **Avoid being closer to one wall of the room than the other.** If one speaker is closer to one side wall than the other, once again you'll get a totally different frequency response between the two because of phase and reflection issues. It's best to set up directly in the center of the room if possible. Symmetry is essential to keep a balanced stereo image with a stable frequency response in the room. That means that your sweet spot will be in the exact center of the room if the speakers are exactly the same distance from each side wall. While it may seem tempting to set up some other way, acoustically you could be asking for trouble.

- **Avoid different types of wall absorption.** If one side of the room contains a window and the other is drywall, carpet, or acoustic foam, once again you'll have an unbalanced stereo image because one side will be brighter sounding than the other. Try to make the walls on each sides of the speakers the same material.

- **Make sure you place the speakers on stands.** Speakers mounted directly on a desk or console can defeat the purpose of the acoustic treatment, so speaker stands can really make a big difference in the sound. Mark the position of the speakers with masking tape, and mark the position of one-inch increments up to six inches either way from the wall so you don't have to re-measure in the event that you have to move things. Exact distances are critical, so always use a tape measure because even an inch can make a big difference in the sound.

Exercise Pod: Improving The Listening Environment

E1.1: Play a song that you think sounds great and you're very familiar with.

A) Place your monitors at the 25% point of your room. Does the frequency response change? Are some bass frequencies missing? What happened to the stereo image? Are some bass frequencies reinforced?

B) Move the speakers a few inches backwards from the 25% point. Does the frequency response change? Are some bass frequencies missing? Are some bass frequencies reinforced? Is the response smoother?

C) Move the speakers a few inches forwards from the 25% point. Does the frequency response change? Are some bass frequencies missing? What happened to the stereo image? Are some bass frequencies reinforced? Is the response smoother?

E1.2: A) Now move the speakers so they're only a few inches away from the front wall. Does the frequency response change? Are some bass frequencies missing? What happened to the stereo image? Are some bass frequencies reinforced? Is the response smoother?

E1.3: A) Place one speaker in a corner of the room. Does the frequency response change? Are some bass frequencies missing? Are some bass frequencies reinforced? Is the response smoother?

E1.4: A) If your speaker setup is *not* placed in the exact center of the room, make a mental note as to how it sounds.

B) Now move the speakers to the exact center of the room between the walls. Does the frequency response change? What happened to the stereo image? Are some bass frequencies missing? Are some bass frequencies reinforced? Is the response smoother?

Basic Monitor Setup

Now that your listening position is placed correctly in the room, it's time to set up your monitors. While most home studios seem to have a random amount of space between their monitors, there are a number of general guidelines you can use to optimize your setup. Since most rooms are unique in some way in terms of dimensions or absorbent qualities, you may have to vary from the following outline a little, but these are good places to start from.

- **Check The Distance Between The Monitors.** If the monitors are too close together, the stereo field will lack definition. If the monitors are too far apart, the focal point or "sweet spot" will be too far behind your head and you'll hear the left or the right side individually, but not both together as one. The rule of thumb is that the speakers should be as far apart as their distance from the listening position. That is, if your listening position is four feet away from the monitors, then start by moving them four feet apart so that you make an equilateral triangle between you and the two monitors (Figure 1.4).

- That being said, it's been found that 67 1/2 inches from tweeter to tweeter seems to be an optimum distance between speakers, and focuses the speakers three to six inches behind your head (which is exactly what you want).

- **Check The Angle Of The Monitors.** Not angling the speakers properly will cause smearing of the stereo field, which is a major cause of a lack of instrument definition when you're listening to your mix. The correct angle is somewhat determined by taste, as some mixers prefer the monitors angled directly at their mixing position while others prefer the focal point (the point where the sound from the tweeters converges) anywhere from three to 24 inches behind them to widen the stereo field (see Figure 1.5).

- It's been found over time that an angle of 30 degrees that's focused about 18 inches behind the mixer's head works the best in most cases.

- A great trick for finding the correct angle is to mount a mirror over each tweeter and adjust the speakers so that your face is clearly seen in both mirrors at the same time when you are in your mixing position.

- **Check How The Monitors Are Mounted.** If at all possible, it's best to mount your monitor speakers on stands just directly behind the meter bridge of the console or edge of your desk. This gives you a much smoother frequency response.

- Monitors that are placed directly on top of a computer desk or console meter bridge without using any isolation are subject to low frequency cancellations because the sound travels through the desk or console, through the floor and reaches your ears before

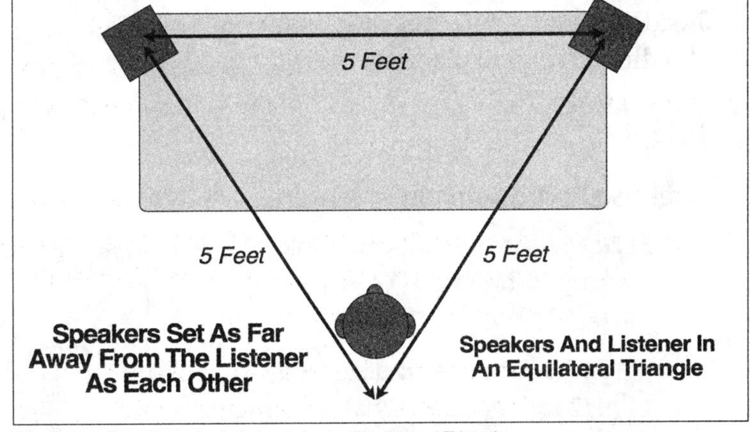

Figure 1.4 Speakers And Listener In An Equilateral Triangle

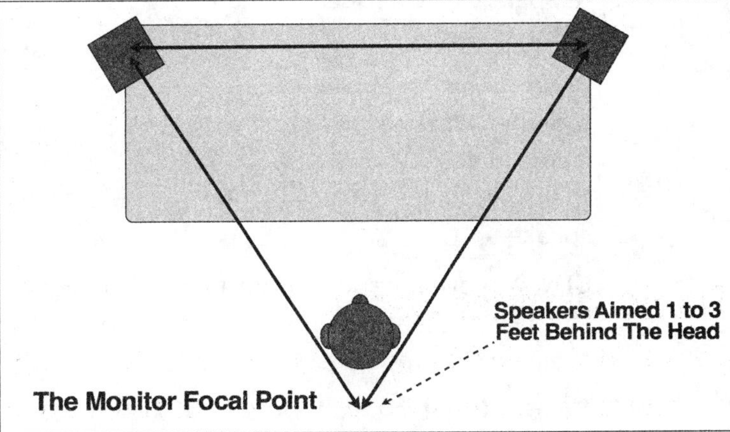

Figure 1.5 The Monitor Focal Point

the direct sound from the monitors through the air gets there. This causes some frequency cancellation and a general smearing effect of the audio. If you must set your speakers on the desk or console, place them on a 1/2 or 3/4 inch piece of open cell neoprene, a thick mouse pad or two, or something like the Prime Acoustic Recoil Stabilizers (see Figure 1.6). You'll be surprised how much better they sound as a result.

• **Check How The Monitor Parameters Are Set.** Almost everyone uses powered monitors these days, but don't forget that many have a few parameter controls either on the front or rear that can change the sound from a little to a lot. Be sure that these are set correctly for the application (make sure you read the manual) and *are set the same on each monitor.*

• **Check The Position Of The Tweeters.** Many monitors are meant to be used in an upright position, yet users frequently will lay them down on their sides. That makes them easier to see over, but the frequency response suffers as a result. That being said, if the speakers are designed to lay on their sides, most mixers prefer that the tweeters be on the outside towards the walls because the stereo field is widened (see Figure 1.7). Sometimes tweeters to the inside works but that usually results in the stereo image smearing. Try it both ways and see which one works best for your application.

• If your speakers are placed upright, be sure that the tweeters are head-height, since the high frequency response at the mixer's position will suffer if they're too high and firing over your head. Sometimes it's necessary to even flip them over and place them on their tops in order to get the proper tweeter height.

Figure 1.6: Yamaha NS-10s On Recoil Stabilizers

Figure 1.7 Speakers With Tweeters To The Outside

Exercise Pod: Speaker Placement

E1.5: Play a song that you think sounds great and you're very familiar with.

A) Place the monitors exactly 67 1/2 inches apart. What does the stereo image sound like? What happens to the frequency balance of the speakers?

B) Now move the speakers closer together. What happens to the stereo image? What happens to the frequency balance of the speakers?

C) Now move the speakers further apart beyond the 67 1/2 inches. What happens to the stereo image? What happens to the frequency balance of the speakers?

E1.6: A) Angle the monitors so that they are pointing directly at the center of your head. What is the stereo image like?

B) Now angle the monitors so that they're aiming at a point about six inches behind your head. What is the stereo image like now?

E1.7: A) If your monitors are sitting on your desk or console, place a mouse pad or two underneath each one. What does it sound like? Did the low end get tighter and more focused? What's the stereo field like?

B) Place the speakers back on the console or desk, but without the mouse pads. Does it sound any different? What's the stereo field like?

C) If you have stands, now place them back on the stands. Does it sound any different? What's the stereo field like?

E1.8: A) If your monitor speakers have parameter controls on the front or back, randomly change the controls on the right speaker. What happens to the frequency response? What happens with the stereo image?

B) Now set the parameter controls so that they're exactly the same on each speaker (including the volume control if there is one). What happens to the stereo image? What happens to the low-end frequency response?

E1.9: A) Lay each speaker down on its side so that the tweeters are positioned to the outside. What happens to the stereo image? What happens to the frequency response?

B) Now flip each speaker so that the tweeters are positioned to the inside. What happens to the stereo image? What happens to the frequency response?

How To Listen

We've been listening to the world around us all of our lives without thinking about it, but when it comes to recording and mixing, we must take our listening ability to another level altogether. The following explanations and exercises are designed to make you think about what you're listening to while recording or mixing, as well as provide you with set of tools to make sure that what you record will fit into the mix later.

Basic Listening Technique

It's time to develop your critical listening skills. All of your life you've been listening to things as a whole. When you were outside in the park, you heard the dogs barking, birds chirping, a police car siren in the distance, children laughing while they're playing; but you've mostly heard it all as one all-encompassing sound and only occasionally zeroed in on a portion of it without realizing it. When you went to a party, you heard the music in the background, guests laughing and talking, ice cubes tinkling in the glass as drinks were being made, and your ears might've picked up a conversation in the distance with a tidbit of juicy gossip. That was the beginning of critical listening, when you zeroed in on just that conversation within the audio din of the evening. When you listened to a song on the radio, you listened to the song as a whole, and never really listened to the individual parts of the mix, unless you heard a particular instrument that you played.

Although when you're recording you might only be listening to a single instrument at a time, it still has to fit into the context of the mix with all of the other instruments. That's why it's important to get a reference point as to how the individual elements works together.

Now it's time to begin to break those sound sculptures down into individual parts. This means identifying individual musical instruments, mix elements, frequency response, mix balance, and ambiance, to name a few. Beware, after you begin to do this, you'll never hear music in the same way again, for better or worse.

Exercise Pod: What To Listen For

Play back one of your favorite songs, but make sure it's available at the highest resolution possible, which means CD, vinyl, or if it's one of your mixes, directly from your DAW. You're going to learn to listen to this mix in a different way.

E1.10: Listen to the mix. How many individual instruments can you identify?

E1.11: Listen to the mix. What part of the frequency spectrum does each instrument or vocal take up?

E1.12: Listen to the mix. How many different types of ambiance (natural or artificial reverb) can you identify? Does each instrument have its own ambiance? Is there one general ambiance that pulls everything together? Does anything have a noticeable delay?

E1.13: Listen to the mix. What is the most interesting thing in the mix? Is it a vocal or an instrument or a sound effect? Is there an effect that catches your ear?

E1.14: Listen to the mix. What is the frequency balance of the mix as a whole like? Are there a lot of high frequencies? Does the song have a deep bottom end?

E1.15: Listen to the mix. Does the song have a lot of dynamics? Does it seemed to be compressed? Can you hear the compression on individual instruments or vocals?

How Loud (Or Soft) Should I Listen?

It's important when recording that you listen at a volume that is sufficiently loud so that all of the frequencies of the recording are properly represented. If it's too quiet, you may find it difficult to gauge the low end properly; if it's too loud, ear fatigue or even hearing damage occurs.

High SPL levels for long periods of time are generally not recommended for the following reasons:

1) First the obvious one: exposure to high volume levels over long periods of time may cause long-term physical damage.

2) High volume levels for long periods of time will not only cause the onset of ear fatigue, but physical fatigue as well. This means that you might effectively be able to work only six hours instead of the normal eight (or 10 or 12) that's possible if listening at lower levels.

3) The ear has different frequency response curves at high volume levels that overcompensate on both the high and low frequencies. This means that your high volume mix will generally sound pretty limp when it's played at softer levels.

4) Balances tend to blur at higher levels. What sounds great at higher levels won't necessarily sound that way when played softer. However, balances that are made at softer levels always work when played louder.

While most mixers will listen at multiple levels (up loud for a minute to check the low end, and moderate while checking the EQ and effects), recording is usually done at a single constant level. Changing the level too much can cause your listening reference point to drift, so you won't be able to gauge the frequency response of what you're recording. Some speakers don't reproduce all frequencies the same at different volumes, so changing listening levels can really fool you as to exactly what you're recording.

Pick a volume level that's comfortably loud, but not too loud, and keep it there for the entire session. You'll find that your recordings will sound better as a result.

CHAPTER 2
THE MICROPHONE

Microphones appear in an almost endless variety of shapes, sizes, design types, and costs, but they all do exactly the same thing: convert acoustic vibrations (in the form of air pressure) to electrical energy so it can be amplified or recorded. There are different methods of mic construction to achieve this, and each one has a bearing on the sound.

Microphone Types

There are three types of microphones, each with a different design philosophy and each with a different sound, which can sometimes make one type work better than another in certain applications. Let's look at the differences.

The Dynamic Microphone

Figure 2.1: A Shure SM58 Dynamic Microphone

Dynamic mics can be made fairly inexpensively and can take a beating without breaking. If you play live you're most likely already familiar with an excellent dynamic microphone: the Shure SM58 (see Figure 2.1), a workhorse for live sound for more than 40 years.

A dynamic microphone gets its name from the fact that sound waves cause movement of a thin metallic diaphragm and an attached coil of wire that "dynamically" moves inside a permanent magnet to change acoustic energy into electronic energy (see

Figure 2.2). This construction gives the dynamic mic its robustness, but because the diaphragm is relatively heavy, it means that it can't respond to sound waves quickly, which means that its high frequency response beyond 10kHz is usually limited.

Most dynamic microphones also exhibit a resonant frequency peak (a frequency or group of frequencies that is emphasized) somewhere around 1k to 4kHz. This resonant response is sometimes called a "presence peak" because it occurs in the frequency region that directly affects voice intelligibility, which makes it a natural for sound reinforcement.

Dynamic Microphone Characteristics

- Robust and durable

- Can be relatively inexpensive

- Insensitive to changes in humidity

- Needs no external or internal power to operate

- Has a resonant peak in the frequency response

- Usually weak high-frequency response beyond 10kHz

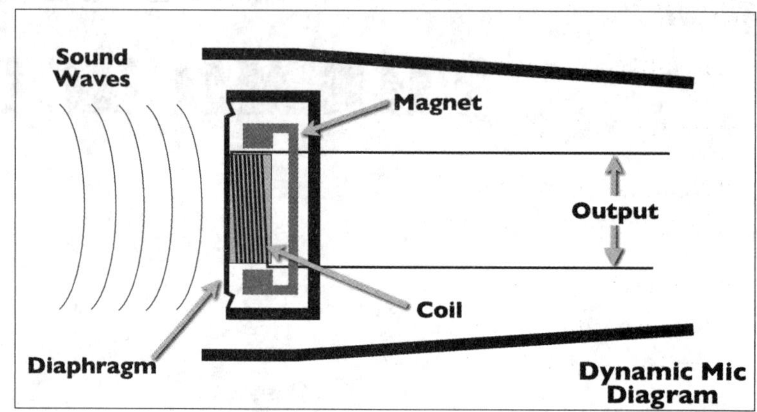

Figure 2.2: Dynamic Mic Block Diagram

Typical Dynamic Microphone Applications

- Sound reinforcement

- Snare drum miking

- Guitar miking

- Voice-overs and broadcast

Dynamic Microphone Examples

- Shure SM57, SM58, and PG57

- AKG D-112

- Sennheiser MD421

- Heil PR-40

- Audix i5

The Ribbon Microphone

The ribbon microphone operates almost the same as the dynamic microphone, but uses a strip of extremely thin aluminum foil as a diaphram instead of a relatively heavy coil of wire (see Figure 2.3). This means that it moves quickly in response to acoustic sound, which also means that it has great high frequency response as a result. The problem is that the foil is so thin that the mic has a weaker output signal than a dynamic as a result. Ribbon mics also have a smoother response than a dynamic since they don't have a mid-range presence peak.

The biggest downside to using ribbon mics is that they're fragile because of the thinness of the aluminum diaphragm (see Figure 2.4). The air blast from a vocal, kick drum, or even slamming the protective case will pop it so fast (some mics are more immune than others) that you won't even realize it until it's too late. That's why ribbons always have to be used with a little caution, but it's worth it because they sound great.

Ribbon Microphone Characteristics

- Relatively flat frequency response
- Better high frequency response compared to dynamics
- Needs no external or internal power to operate
- Somewhat fragile and requires care during operation and handling
- Moderately expensive

Typical Ribbon Microphone Applications

- Overheads or cymbal miking
- Bass miking
- Piano miking
- Electric or acoustic guitar miking
- Brass miking

Ribbon Microphone Examples

- Royer R-101 and 121
- RCA 44BX and 77DX
- Cascade FAT HEAD
- Audio Technica AT4080 and 4081
- MXL R144

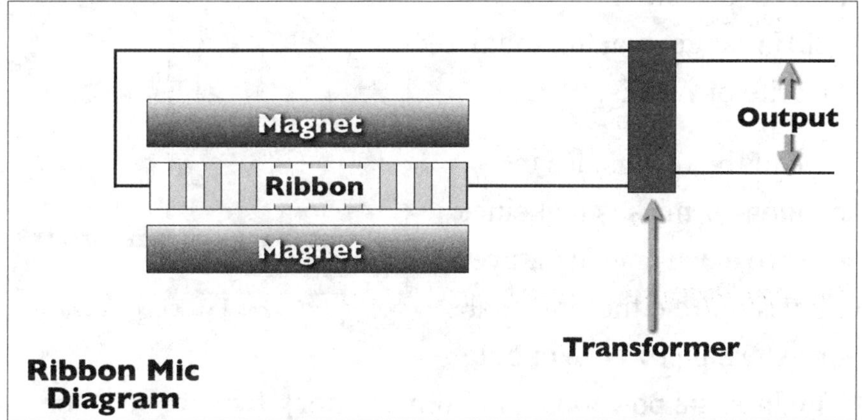

Figure 2.3: Ribbon Mic Block Diagram

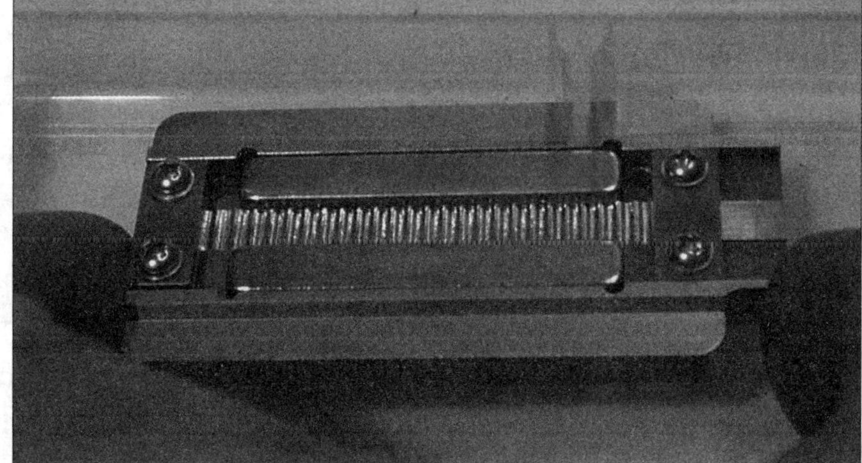

Figure 2.4: Ribbon Mic Transducer
Courtesy of Royer Labs

The Condenser Microphone

The condenser microphone works on the same principle as both dynamic and ribbon mics, but takes a different approach. All condensers use two electrically charged plates, one that can move, which acts as a diaphragm, and one that's fixed (see Figure 2.5). Because the sound wave is varying an electric charge instead of moving a diaphragm through a magnet, it can respond faster and therefore have a better high frequency response and the ability to capture sounds with very quick attack times, like drums and cymbals.

Condenser mics come in what's known as small diaphragm and large diaphragm versions. The small diaphragm versions have a single pickup pattern, while the large diaphragm versions have multiple pickup patterns. The small diaphragm versions also usually have a slightly lower frequency response while the large diaphragm versions have a presence peak in the 8k to 12kHz range, making them a favorite of vocalists.

One of the downsides to condenser mics is that since they're electronic in nature, they require either internal or external power to operate.

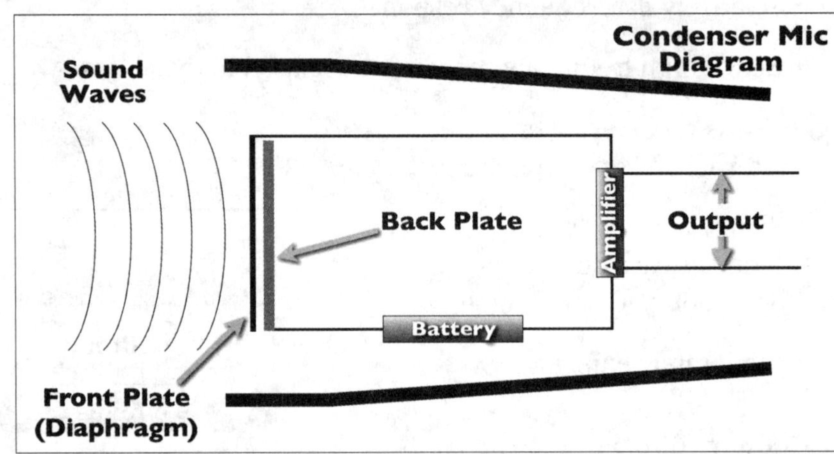

Figure 2.5: Condenser Mic Block Diagram

The internal power comes from a battery (which, because of its low voltage, usually limits the amount of output level the mic can produce), but most condensers are powered either from a power source called *Phantom Power* (which can be found on all recording consoles and most preamps), or an external power supply. Most of the old vintage Neumann, Sony, and AKG condenser mics actually used vacuum tubes inside (which is another reason why they were so large), which required a very large and expensive power supply.

In the past most condenser mics were very expensive, but today you can buy a small diaphragm condenser for less than $100 from a number of manufacturers. The problem with these cheaper mics is that the quality control isn't that stringent, so while it's possible to get a great one, it's also possible to get one that has a frequency response like a bumpy road filled with potholes. The trouble is, you never know what you'll get. Try to listen to it before you purchase, or just save your money and buy a quality brand.

Condenser Microphone Characteristics

- Excellent low and high frequency response
- Good ones are somewhat expensive

- Requires external powering

- Large diaphragm models can be relatively bulky

- Low cost models can suffer from poor or inconsistent frequency response

- Humidity and temperature affects performance

Typical Condenser Microphone Applications

- Overheads or cymbal miking

- Drum miking

- Piano miking

- Acoustic guitar miking

- Vocal miking

- String section miking

Condenser Microphone Examples

- Neumann U-87, U-67, U-47

- AKG C12, 414 series, 460

- Shure KSM series

- Mojave Audio MA-100 and 200

- Audio Technica 4033, 4040, and 4047

- MXL V63 and 909

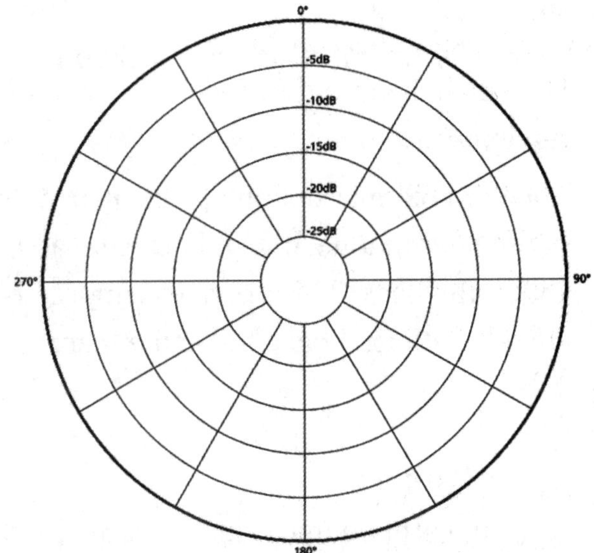

Figure 2.6: A Typical Polar Pattern

Microphone Directional Response

The directional response (sometimes called polar pattern) of a microphone is the way the microphone responds to sounds coming from different directions around it. This is determined by the way the case of the mic is designed, and in a condenser mic, the number of diaphragms it contains.

The directional response of a microphone is recorded on what's known as a polar diagram and is sometimes described as the "polar pattern." This polar diagram shows the signal pick-up level (sometimes shown in decibels) from all angles and at different frequency ranges (see Figure 2.6). To make matters a bit more confusing, all mics have different polar patterns at different frequencies. While a mic can be very directional at one frequency (usually the higher frequencies), it can be virtually non-directional, or omnidirectional, at another.

The reason why the polar response is important is it determines how the mic can be used, which can make a huge difference in multi-microphone settings where leakage from different sound sources can be a problem.

There are four typical patterns commonly found in microphone design.

Omnidirectional

An omni-directional microphone picks up sound equally from all directions. That doesn't mean that the frequency response is equal in all directions, though, so it's still best to point an omni directly at the sound source for the most accurate pickup (see Figure 2.7).

Cardioid

The cardioid microphone picks up best from the front of the microphone, but still picks up a bit to the side and to the back. This provides a more-or-less heart-shaped pattern, hence the name "cardioid" (see Figure 2.8).

Hyper-Cardioid

A hyper-cardioid mic is just a more directional version of a cardioid mic. That means it's even less sensitive to sounds coming from the sides, but does pick up a bit from the rear (see Figure 2.9).

Figure Eight

Figure eight or bi-directional microphones pickup almost equally in the front and back, but nearly nothing to each side. The frequency response is usually slightly better on the front side of the microphone so it sounds a bit brighter from that direction. A figure eight mic can be very useful when a high degree of sound rejection is required (see Figure 2.10).

Proximity Effect

Cardioid and hyper-cardioid microphones experience a low frequency build-up the closer the mic is placed to the source, which is known as "proximity effect." As a result, a mic that's placed within a couple of inches from the source (like on a guitar amp or snare drum) will seem to have a lot more bottom end than if placed a

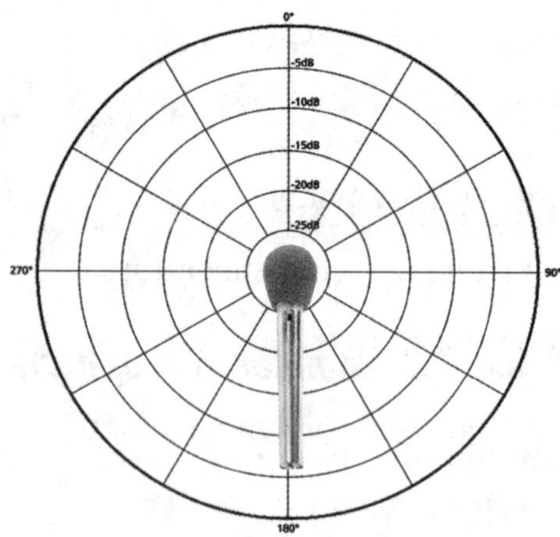

Figure 2.7: Omni-Directional Polar Pattern

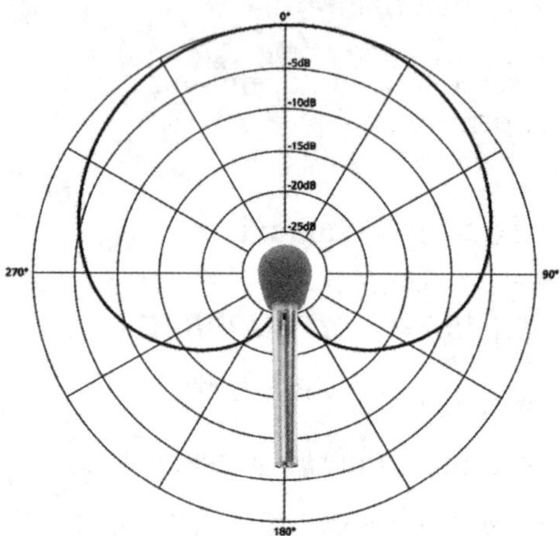

Figure 2.8: Cardioid Polar Pattern

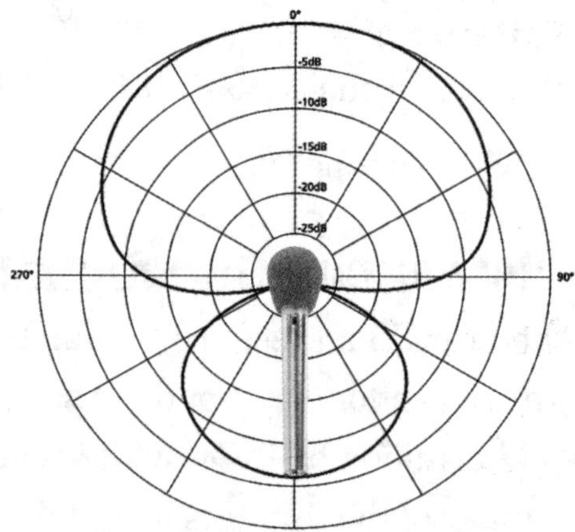

Figure 2.9: Hyper-Cardioid Polar Pattern

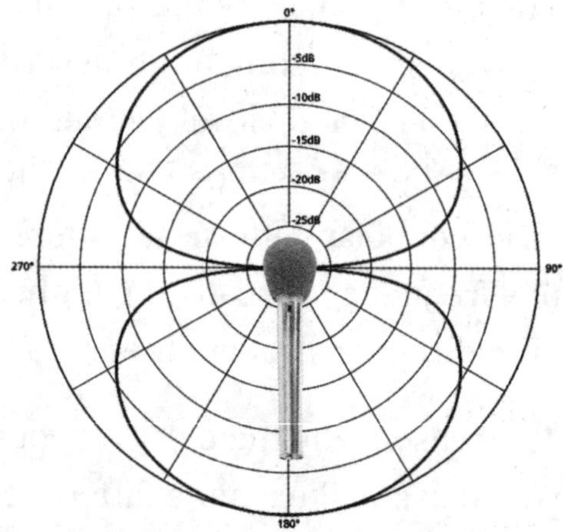

Figure 2.10: Figure Eight Polar Pattern

foot or more away. Sometimes this can be useful for adding fullness to the source, but it can also make the frequency response seem out of balance if it is not taken into account.

Microphone Controls

While dynamic and ribbon microphones may be limited to only a single rolloff filter control (if that), condenser mics may have a few more.

High-Pass or Rolloff Filter

Because microphones can sometimes capture low frequency sounds like truck rumble and machinery noise that add nothing to the audio, a rolloff filter is frequently added to help eliminate the problem. The rolloff point can be from anywhere from 40 to 100Hz, but more often than not, 60Hz is selected.

-10 or -20dB Pad

Many condenser microphones have much more output than dynamic or ribbon mics to begin with, but when coupled with a loud sound source like a snare drum the output can be so hot that it overloads the microphone preamp that it's connected to. A -10 or -20 attenuation pad decreases the output signal by that amount in order to keep whatever electronics the mic's plugged into from overloading.

Pattern Selector

Most large diaphragm condenser microphones are capable of multiple pickup patterns, which are selected by the pickup selector. Some are switchable from one pattern to another, while others are continuously variable.

Microphone Accessories

There are some microphone accessories that are nearly essential in certain applications. Here are a few.

Pop Filters

Pop filters or screens are designed to eliminate the blasts of wind when a vocalists sings "P's" and "B's" (see Figure 2.11). These screens can be of limited value, however, when in fact positioning and vocal/microphone technique are far more useful in reducing these "pops."

Spitting on a valuable mic is a really big reason to use a pop screen though. Condensation coming from a vocalist's breath can cause a condenser

Figure 2.11: Gotham DUA0040 Pop Filter

microphone to actually stop working for a short time, and the pop filter goes a long way to eliminate the problem.

External pop screens are designed to be as acoustically transparent as possible, but they usually have a slight effect on the high frequency response of the mic. For instance, a Neumann U87 style windscreen will knock the response at 15kHz down about 2 to 3 dB, which may or may not be heard depending upon the arrangement of the song.

Although there are many models of pop filters available commercially, it's fairly easy to build your own. Buy an embroidery hoop and some pantyhose, cut a leg of hose until you have roughly a square sheet, clamp it in the embroidery hoop, then place it between the mic and singer.

A lot of people affix pop filters to a gooseneck device that attaches to the boom stand that holds the mic. It's usually easier to mount to pop filter on a second boom as it makes positioning less frustrating and more exact.

Shock Mounts

Shock Mounts are designed to prevent the microphone from picking up transmission noises that come through the mic stand (see Figure 2.12), such as footsteps or the rumble from traffic outside. Large diaphragm mics are usually a lot more susceptible to mechanical noise than small diaphragm ones, which is why a shock mount is usually provided in the package. One of the downsides to using a shock mount

Figure 2.12: A typical Shock Mount

is that in order to provide the best isolation, it has to hold the mic clamp with rubber bands. This can make it somewhat difficult to position the mic as a result.

Exercise Pod: The Microphone

E2.1: Microphone Types

A) Set a dynamic mic up to listen to any sound source. Are there a lot of high frequencies? Are there a lot of low frequencies? Note how loud the level is.

B) Set a ribbon mic up to listen to the same sound source. How is the sound different? Are there more high frequencies? Are there more low frequencies? Is the ribbon mic louder or softer than the dynamic mic?

C) Set a condenser mic up to listen to the same sound source. How is the sound different? Are there more high frequencies? Are there more low frequencies? Is the condenser mic louder or softer than the ribbon or dynamic mic?

E2.2: Microphone Directional Patterns

A) Set a directional mic up so it's pointing directly at a sound source. Are there a lot of high frequencies? Are there a lot of low frequencies? Note how loud the level is.

B) Now turn the mic 90 degrees to the sound source. How is the sound different? Are there more high frequencies? Are there more low frequencies? Is the mic louder or softer than when pointed directly at the sound source?

C) Now turn the mic 180 degrees to the sound source so the back of the mic is facing it. How is the sound different? Are there more high frequencies? Are there more low frequencies? Is the mic louder or softer than when pointed directly at the sound source?

D) Set an omnidirectional mic up so it's pointing directly at same sound source. How is the sound different? Are there more high frequencies? Are there more low frequencies? Is it louder or softer than the directional mic?

E) Now turn the mic 90 degrees to the sound source. How is the sound different? Are there more high frequencies? Are there more low frequencies? Is the mic louder or softer than when pointed directly at the sound source?

F) Now turn the mic 180 degrees to the sound source so the back of the mic is facing it. How is the sound different? Are there more high frequencies? Are there more low frequencies? Is the mic louder or softer than when pointed directly at the sound source?

G) Set a figure eight mic up so it's pointing directly at same sound source. How is the sound different? Are there more high frequencies? Are there more low frequencies? Is it louder or softer than the directional mic?

H) Now turn the mic 90 degrees to the sound source. How is the sound different? Are there more high frequencies? Are there more low frequencies? Is the mic louder or softer than when pointed directly at the sound source?

I) Now turn the mic 180 degrees to the sound source so the back of the mic is facing it. How is the sound different? Are there more high frequencies? Are there more low frequencies? Is the mic louder or softer than when pointed directly at the sound source?

E2.3: Microphone Proximity Effect

A) Set a directional mic up so it's pointing directly at a sound source from a distance of about three feet. Are there a lot of high frequencies? Are there a lot of low frequencies? Note how loud the level is.

B) Move the mic closer so it's only about a foot away. Are there a more high frequencies? Are there more low frequencies? Is it louder than before?

C) Set an omnidirectional mic up so it's pointing directly at a sound source from a distance of about three feet. Are there a lot of high frequencies? Are there a lot of low frequencies? Note how loud the level is.

D) Move the mic closer so it's only about a foot away. Are there a more high frequencies? Are there more low frequencies? Is it louder than before? How does it differ in sound from the directional mic?

E) Move the mic closer so it's only about an inch away. Are there a more high frequencies? Are there more low frequencies? Is it louder than before? How does it differ in sound from the directional mic?

E2.4: Microphone Pop Filters

> A) Set a directional mic about six inches in front of a vocalist or speaker. Have the singer or speaker sing or talk using words with "P's," "B's," and "S's." Can you hear any air blasts that pop the mic?
>
> B) Set a pop filter about half way between the mic and the singer and have him repeat the previous exercise. Can you still hear any air blasts? Is there any change in the high frequency response?
>
> C) Move the microphone back to about a foot away from the speaker or vocalist and have him repeat the exercise. Can you still hear any air blasts? Is there any change in the high frequency response?

Direct Boxes

Direct Injection (DI, or "going direct") of a signal means that a microphone is bypassed, and an electric instrument is plugged directly into the console, microphone preamp, or recording device. It's used to capture the pure sound of the instrument (which isn't always desirable), and to eliminate the need for an additional microphone, making the session setup faster.

There are a couple of other good reasons why a direct box is used, though. Have you ever tried to plug your guitar or keyboard directly into the XLR jack of a microphone preamp without the direct box? What happens is that there's an impedance mismatch that changes the frequency response of the instrument (although it won't hurt anything), usually causing the high frequencies to drop off and making the instrument sound dull. The DI matches the impedance so the frequency response is not affected, and also provides ground isolation to eliminate hum and allow for long cable runs.

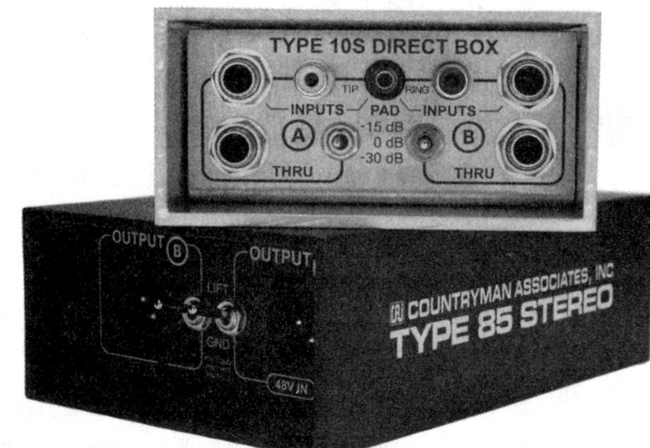

Figure 2.13: A Countryman Type 85 Active Stereo Direct Box
Courtesy of Countryman Electronics

Direct Box Types

There are two basic types of direct boxes: active (which provides gain and therefore needs electronics requiring either battery, AC, or phantom power) and passive (which has no gain and doesn't require power). An active box like the Countryman Type 85 (see Figure 2.13) sometimes has enough gain to be able to actually replace the mic amp and connect directly to a storage device like a tape machine or DAW.

Figure 2.14: Radial JDI Passive Direct Box
Courtesy of Radial Engineering

Passive direct boxes are generally a lot cheaper than active units, but the cheaper they are, the more the low frequency response usually suffers, which is not the best thing for recording an electric bass. An excellent DI that's not too expensive is made by Radial Engineering and called their JDI direct box (see Figure 2.14).

Amplifier Emulators

The amplifier emulator, which is basically a glorified active direct box, has been around for some time now and has become a staple of just about

Figure 2.15: An Amplifier Emulator: Line 6 Guitar Pod Pro
Courtesy of Line 6

any studio (see Figure 2.15). An emulator attempts to electronically duplicate the sound of different guitar and bass amplifiers, speaker cabinets, and even miking schemes. The advantages of an emulator is that it provides a quick and easy setup, gives a very wide tonal variation, and provides the proper interface to just about any recording device. While they might not sound as realistic as a properly miked amplifier in a great studio with a terrific signal chain, they can provide a more than adequate substitute if you don't have any of those pieces available.

CHAPTER 3
BASIC RECORDING GEAR

The typical gear needed for recording need not be elaborate or expensive in order to get a great result. Knowing what gear works for a particular situation and how to drive it makes all the difference in the world. Let's look at the various components of a typical recording signal path.

The Microphone Preamplifier

Almost as important as the microphone is the microphone preamplifier, or "mic pre," "mic amp," or just "preamp." This circuit boosts the tiny output voltage from the microphone up to a level (called "Line Level") easily sent around the studio to consoles, outboard gear, and DAWs.

Nearly all consoles and many DAW interfaces have mic preamps built into them, but in most cases the quality of the circuitry that they use isn't nearly as high as what's available in a dedicated outboard piece. Also, each mic pre has its own sound, and most engineers will select the mic pre and microphone combination because of the the color the combination provides, which makes the captured audio fit the music better.

Why A Separate Mic Amp?

Usually a dedicated mic amp sounds a lot better than the ones included in a DAW interface and console. An outboard pre generally provides a signal that has higher highs and lower lows (meaning it has better frequency response), and is clearer and cleaner. This increased quality comes at a price, as an outboard mic pre can cost anywhere from $100 (which is very inexpensive) to several thousand dollars per channel. As a comparison, a mic amp on a cheap interface frequently costs less than $2. As with everything, you get what you pay for.

Microphone Preamp Controls

Mic Preamps do only one job and that's amplify. As a result, they usually don't have that many controls, although the more expensive, exotic models might have some extra features. The two items that every pre has in common is a Gain control (sometimes called "Trim") and some type of overload indicator. Other controls that you might see are output gain, impedance, input pad, phase, phantom powering, hi-pass filter, and extensive metering.

The primary controls on a mic preamp are:

Gain, Level, Trim

Gain controls how much the microphone signal is amplified (see Figure 3.1). Most mic preamps have about 60 dB of gain (which amplifies the mic signal a million times), but some have as much as 80 dB to accommodate low output ribbon microphones or field audio recording in which the signals captured by the mic are extremely quiet.

Metering

Metering on a mic preamp can be as simple as a single LED indicator that signals an overload, to a full-on ladder-style LED peak meter, as found on consoles or DAWs (see Figure 3.1).

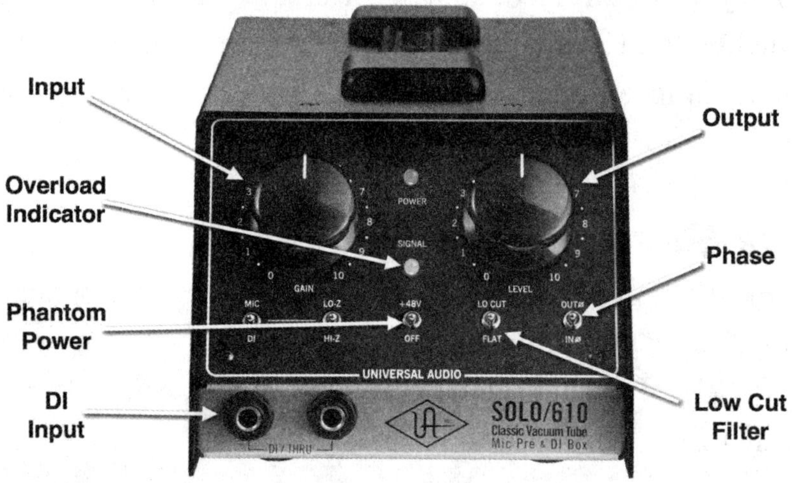

Figure 3.1: Typical Mic Pre Controls On A Universal Audio Solo/610

Input Pad, Pad, Attenuation

The *Pad* is usually a switch that attenuates the signal coming from the microphone anywhere from 10 to 20 dB (it's different for every mic pre) to keep the input circuitry of the mic preamp from overloading (see Figure 3.1). It's used when the mic is trying to capture a very loud sound source, like a snare drum or loud electric guitar.

Phase Switch

The *Phase Switch* changes the polarity of the microphone signal due to either a misplaced or mis-wired microphone. Set the switch to the position that has the most low end (see Figure 3.1). For more on phase, see Chapter 4.

High-Pass Filter/Low-Cut Filter

The *High-Pass Filter* allows only the high frequencies to pass, which means the the low frequencies are attenuated (which is why it's sometimes called a *Low-Cut Filter*). The frequencies that are attenuated are usually anywhere from 40Hz to 160Hz. They're cut off in order to eliminate unwanted low frequency noise like the rumble from heavy truck traffic (see Figure 3.1). On most preamps, this frequency is fixed, but on many models it's variable.

Phantom Power, 48V

It was pointed out in Chapter 2 that condenser microphones need some sort of power in order to operate. Mic preamps and recording consoles frequently supply that power (see Figure 3.1), which is a standard 48 volts, and that's why sometimes it's just labeled as "48V." This is called phantom power, and it's a pretty standard feature on most dedicated mic pres.

Instrument Input, Hi-Z, DI

Almost all mic preamps that are made these days have an input where you can plug an electric instrument like a guitar or bass to turn the unit into an active direct box. It's sometimes marked as "Hi-Z" because it's a high impedance input that's specifically matched to these kinds of instruments.

Setting Up The Mic Preamp

The best way to set the a mic preamp up is to adjust the *Gain* control until the clip LED flashes only on the loudest sections of the recording. In most cases, the overload indicator doesn't actually light at the onset of clipping, so it's OK if it flashes occasionally (but check the manual first to make sure that's what really happens instead of it indicating the onset

of an overload). This gives you the best combination of low noise with the least distortion (unless, of course, you like distortion). If you set the gain of the mic amp too low, you might have to raise the gain at another place in the signal chain, which can raise the noise as well.

After the correct signal level is reached, insert the *High-Pass Filter* to eliminate unwanted low frequencies. On frequencies where you really want to capture these low frequencies, like kick drum, bass, or floor tom, don't insert it.

Figure 3.2: A Daking Mic Pre One Microphone Preamp

Exercise Pod: Setting Up The Mic Preamp

E3.1: A) Place a mic on a sound source. Adjust the *Gain* control of the preamp until the clip LED just flashes only on the loudest sections of the recording, then back it off. Is the sound distorted? Is it noisy when the instrument isn't playing?

B) Select the *Input Pad*. Is the sound louder or softer? Is the sound distorted? Is it noisy when the instrument isn't playing? Select the position of the Input Pad so you can set the *Gain* control about mid-way.

C) Select the *Phase Switch*. Can you hear a difference in the sound? You shouldn't unless there are other microphones set up on the same instrument.

D) Insert the *High-Pass Filter*. Did the sound change? Is it cleaner? Did the low end change? If the filter doesn't change the low end much, leave it inserted.

Compressors/Limiters

A compressor is nothing more than an automated level control that uses the input signal to determine the output level. Some models do this so transparently that you can't hear them working at all, while other models impart their own sound by just being inserted into the signal path. Regardless of how they sound, all have roughly the same parameter controls and are operated the same way.

Compressor Controls

Not every compressor has the same controls, although most of the modern hardware and plug-in models are starting to all have a similar parameter setup. Let's look at these typical parameter controls.

Ratio

The *Ratio* parameter controls how much the output level of the compressor will increase compared to the level being fed to the input (see Figure 3.3). For instance, if the compression ratio is set at 4:1 (four to one), that means for every 4 dB of level that goes into the compressor, only 1 dB will come out once the signal reaches the threshold level

Figure 3.3: Typical Compressor Controls

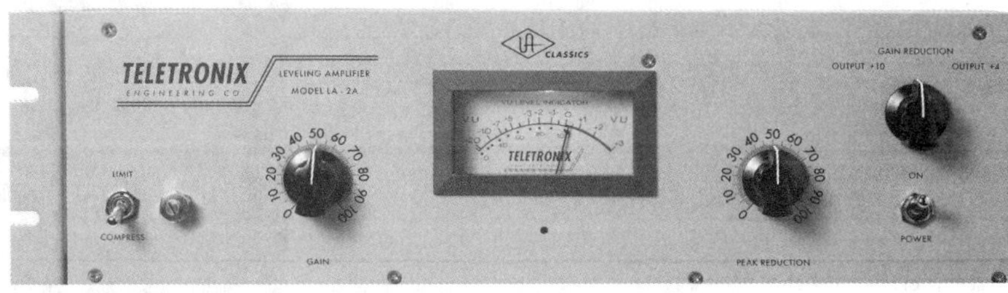
Figure 3.4: A UREI/Teletronix LA-2A Compressor

(the point at which the compressor begins to work). If a compression ratio is set at 8:1, then for every 8 dB that go into the unit, only 1 dB will come out of the output. On some compressors, the ratio control is fixed, but on most compressors the *Ratio* parameter is variable from 1:1 (where there's no compression) to as much as 100:1 (where it then become a limiter, a subject that we'll address later in this chapter). Some compressors (like the famous UREI LA-2A—see Figure 3.4—and LA-3) have a fixed ratio that gives it a particular sound.

Threshold

The *Threshold* control determines the signal level at which the compression begins (see Figure 3.3). Below the threshold point, no compression occurs. For instance, many compressors are calibrated in dB, so a setting of -5 dB means that when the level reaches -5 dB on the input meter, the compression begins to kick in.

Attack And Release

Figure 3.5: dbx 160a Compressor

Most, but not all, compressors have *Attack* and *Release* parameter controls (see Figure 3.3). These controls determine how fast or slow the compressor reacts to the beginning (the attack) and end (the release) of the signal envelope. Many compressors have an *Auto* mode that automatically sets the attack and release according to the dynamics of the signal. Although *Auto* works relatively well, it still doesn't allow you

Figure 3.6: 4 dB Of Compression

to dial in the precise settings required by certain sources. Some compressors (like the famous dbx 160 series—pictured in Figure 3.5) have a fixed attack and release that can't be altered, which helps give the compressor a distinctive sound.

The *Attack* and *Release* controls are the key to proper compressor setup, but many engineers overlook these controls completely. It's possible to get good results by keeping these controls set to the mid-way position, but learning how to use them provides much more consistent and professional results. We'll cover this soon.

Gain, Make-up Gain, Output

When a compressor actually compresses the signal, the level is decreased, so there needs to be another parameter that boosts the signal back up to where it was before it was compressed. Depending upon the compressor, this parameter control is called either *Gain*, *Make-Up Gain*, or *Output* (see Figure 3.3). On some compressors, the amount of make-up gain is automatically determined by the amount of compression used, so the control is eliminated.

Gain Reduction Meter

The gain reduction meter is an indicator of just how much compression is occurring at any given moment (see Figure 3.3). On most devices this is shown via a VU or peak meter that reads backwards. In other words, it's set at zero and usually travels to the left into the minus range to show compression. As an example, a meter that reads -4 dB indicates that there is 4 dB of compression occurring at that time (see Figure 3.6)

Bypass

Most compressors, especially most of the plug-in versions, have a *Bypass* control that allows you to hear the signal without any gain reduction taking place. This is useful to help you hear how much the compressor is controlling or changing the sound, or to make it easy to set the *Output* control so the compressed signal is the same level as the uncompressed signal.

Limiting

While a compressor increases the low levels and decreases the high levels to even out the dynamic range, a limiter keeps the level from ever going much louder once it hits the threshold. It's very much like a truck with a speed governor on it that keeps the speed at 60 mph regardless of how much more you press down on the gas pedal. With a limiter, once you hit the predetermined signal level, it never gets much louder no matter how much more input level it receives.

A compressor and a limiter are somewhat the same except for the ratio setting. Any time the compression ratio is set to 10:1 or more, it's considered a limiter. Limiting is usually used in sound reinforcement for speaker protection (there are some internal limiters on powered studio monitors as well), but is used also during recording to make sure that the instrument you're recording doesn't overload.

Compressor/Limiter Setup

There are two things that are important in setting up a compressor: the timing of the *Attack* and *Release*, and the amount of compression. Here are a few simple steps to help you set one up. *Remember: the idea is to make the compressor breathe in time with the song.*

1. With a signal present, start with the attack time set as slow as possible, and release time set as fast as possible on the compressor.

2. Turn the attack faster until the instrument begins to sound a bit dull (this happens because you're compressing the attack portion of the sound envelope). Stop increasing the attack time at this point and even back it off a little.

3. Adjust the release time so that the volume goes back to 90 to 100 percent normal with the pulse of the song. In other words, the release should timed so the instrument breathes with the pulse of the song.

4. When in doubt, set the attack and release times to mid-way and leave them there.

We'll cover a number of compression/limiter exercises in Chapter 4.

Equalizers

While it might not be the best idea to grab the EQ to try to get a good sound while you're recording (at least not at first), it's important to understand what the EQ can do and how it does it.

EQ Parameters

There are a number of parameters that you'll find on most equalizers (see Figure 3.7).

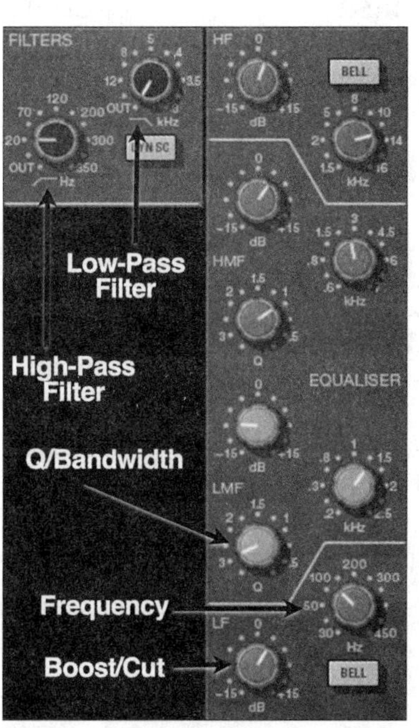

Figure 3.7: The Controls Of A Typical Equalizer

• **Frequency:** The *Frequency* control selects the center frequency around which the equalizer operates, and comes in many forms (see Figure 3.7). It can be a fixed frequency like the tone controls on a car radio or guitar amplifier, selectable frequencies in which a button or detent selects the frequency, or a variable or swept frequency control in which you can continuously select the frequency that's appropriate.

• **Boost/Cut:** This is the control that adds or subtracts the volume of the particular frequency, or band of frequencies, chosen (see Figure 3.7).

• **Q, Bandwidth:** This control selects the band of frequencies that the equalizer will boost or cut. A Q set on 10 will only affect a narrow number of frequencies around the frequency selected, so it's very precise and excellent for cutting an offensive frequency spike (see Figure 3.7). A Q of 2 affects several octaves above and below the center frequency (if 1,000 is selected, it may effect everything from 500Hz through 2,000Hz). The *Q* or *Bandwidth* control is not found on all equalizers.

• **High-Pass Filter/Low-Cut:** The high-pass filter (sometimes abbreviated "HPF") allows high frequencies to pass and cuts off low frequencies (see Figure 3.7). Sometimes the HPF (also sometimes more appropriately called "Low-Cut" because the low frequencies are filtered) has a fixed frequency like at 40 or 60Hz, sometimes there are several frequencies that are selectable, and sometimes the frequency selection is continuously variable.

• **Low-Pass Filter/High-Cut:** The low-pass filter (sometimes abbreviated "LPF") allows low frequencies to pass and cuts off high frequencies (see Figure 3.7). Sometimes the LPF (also sometimes more appropriately called "High-Cut" because the high frequencies are filtered) has a fixed frequency like 10k or 12kHz, sometimes there are several frequencies that are selectable, and sometimes the frequency selection is continuously variable.

• **In/Out:** *In* inserts the equalizer into the circuit while *Out* bypasses it (see Figure 3.7).

A Description Of The Audio Bands

The audio bandwidth is made up of six distinct frequency bands. Each one has an enormous impact on the final sound, so it's important to know the characteristics of each before we begin to use the equalizer.

Frequency Band	Description	Consequences
Sub-Bass **16Hz to 60Hz**	Sounds that are often felt more than heard. They give the music a sense of power	Too much emphasis in this range makes the music sound muddy. Attenuating this range (especially below 40Hz) can clean a mix up considerably.
Bass **60Hz to 250Hz**	Contains the fundamental notes of the rhythm section	EQing this range can make the musical balance either fat or thin. Too much boost in this range can make the music sound boomy.
Low Mids **250Hz to 2kHz**	Contains the low harmonics of most musical instruments	Can introduce a telephone-like quality to the music if boosted too much. Boosting the 500 to 1000Hz octave makes the instruments sound horn-like. Boosting the 1 to 2kHz octave makes them sound tinny. Excess output in this range can cause listening fatigue.
High Mids **2k to 4kHz**	Controls the speech recognition sounds of "M," "B," and "V"	Too much boost in this range, especially at 3kHz, can introduce a lisping quality to a voice. Too much boost in this range can cause listening fatigue. Dipping the 3kHz range on instrument backgrounds and slightly peaking 3kHz on vocals can make the vocals audible without having to decrease the instrumental level in mixes where the voice would otherwise seem buried.

Figure 3.8: Audio Band Description

Frequency Band	Description	Consequences
Presence **4k to 6kHz**	Responsible for the clarity and definition of voices and instruments	Boosting this range can make the music seem closer to the listener. Reducing the 5kHz content of a mix makes the sound more distant and transparent.
Brilliance **6k to 16kHz**	Controls the brilliance and clarity of sounds	Too much emphasis in this range can produce sibilance on the vocals.

Figure 3.8: Audio Band Description (continued)

Equalizer Setup

There are many different methods for EQing an instrument or vocal, but here's a tried and true technique that will never steer you wrong and will keep you from a typical affliction, over-EQing.

Subtractive Equalization

While it's natural to believe that by adding some EQ here and there you'll make the instrument or vocal sound better, that's not necessarily the case. There's a very effective EQ technique called "subtractive equalization" that works by attenuating frequencies instead of boosting them. Many superstar engineers love this method because it makes the sound of the instrument more natural than if you boosted any of its frequencies. This is because every time you boost an EQ, there's a slight amount of a form of distortion called phase shift that's added to the signal as a byproduct of the way an electronic equalizer works. By using subtractive equalization, you completely avoid this artifact. As a result, the track is better able to blend with the others.

Here's how to use subtractive equalization:

1. Set the *Boost/Cut* control to a moderate level of *cut* (8 or 10 dB should work.)

2. Sweep through the frequencies until you find the frequency in which the sound has the least amount of boxiness and the most definition.

3. Adjust the amount of cut to taste. Be aware that too much cut makes the sound thinner.

Alternately, you can try a different approach.

1. Set the *Boost/Cut* control to a moderate level of *boost* (8 or 10 dB should work.)

2. Sweep through the frequencies until you find the frequency that really leaps out above all others. That's the frequency to *cut*.

3. Adjust the amount of cut to taste. Be aware that too much cut makes the sound thinner.

Sometimes you want to be sure that the instrument has a lot of definition. To do that, you can go a few steps further:

> 4. Add some "point" to sound by adding a slight amount (start with only a couple of dB, then add more to taste) of upper midrange (1k to 4kHz).

> 5. If required, add some "sparkle" to sound by adding a slight amount of high frequencies (5k to 10kHz).

> 6. If required, add some "air" to sound by adding a slight amount of the brilliance frequencies (10k to 15kHz).

We'll cover a number of EQ exercises in Chapter 4.

DAW Recording

It's difficult to find a musician who doesn't have some type of recording capability at home these days. It's so easy to put together the kind of studio that you could only dream about a few years ago, so now just about everyone can get in the recording game at very little cost. But there are a few concerns beyond microphone choice and placement that you need to address before you hit the record button.

Getting Sound Into The Computer

In the days of recording consoles and tape machines (and in those studios that still have those units today) recording was actually a little easier than what you find in a typical DAW these days. What you heard in the headphones or on the speakers was always in sync thanks to the miracle of analog (I say that in jest, of course). You still had to deal with getting a signal to the headphones and setting up a cue mix, but you still have those kinds of issue in the digital domain as well.

The Computer Interface

Besides the mic and microphone preamp, the next most important devices that have an impact on the sound quality are the analog to digital converter (abbreviated "ADC"), which is a unit that converts the analog signals into the digital language of the DAW, and the digital to analog converter (abbreviated "DAC"), which is a unit that converts the digital signal back to analog for playback. In most lower end DAW interfaces by manufacturers like Avid, M-Audio, and MOTU, the ADCs and the DACs are built into the same box along with the mic preamps (see Figure 3.9). As you get into higher end systems like Protools|HD, the ADCs and DACs are in separate higher quality units capable of greater fidelity, and specialized outboard units capable of even higher fidelity are available from a number of manufacturers, like Apogee and Lavry.

The fact of the matter is that most converters sold today even at a budget all-in-the-same-box price sound pretty good compared to what was available in the 90s when digital recording was in its infancy. That being said, most DAW software now allows you to mix and match the hardware to the level of quality that you need and can afford.

Like with most everything else in the audio world, price usually does buy you increased quality, but just how much of that quality you'll actually hear still depends upon the weakest link in your signal path.

Latency

One of the biggest problems in the digital world is the result of latency. Latency is the measure of the time it takes (in milliseconds) for your audio signal to pass through your computer during the recording process. This delay is caused by the fact that your computer has to receive, understand, and process the signal, then send the signal back to the outputs for you to hear.

High latency (which means you hear a note from your DAW way after you play or sing it) is what you want to avoid, especially if you're doing overdubs. High latency means it's taking too long for the audio input to get to the audio output, which results in that lag between the time you play a note and when you hear it. A very small lag time (3 to 6 milliseconds) is tolerable, but anything beyond that creates everything from a phasing sound to a full echo, making it distracting or even impossible to sing or play with.

Figure 3.9: Digidesign M-Box
Courtesy of Avid

The lower your latency, the better your music that you're recording will stay in sync with the music that you're playing back, up to a point. If you try to set the latency parameter too low, the audio stream can break up into random static since the computer doesn't have the time to process it.

The key is to adjust your latency (either through your sound card or interface settings, or through third-party audio drivers) as low as it can go without causing the computer to stutter. How low your latency can be set is dependent upon such factors as computer speed, system bus speed, sound card performance, and system memory. Most computers purchased today are powerful enough that you can get the latency pretty low, but you still have to experiment to find the settings that provide the best performance.

The parameter that most computer audio interfaces use to set the latency is called the "input buffer." The smaller the buffer, the lower the latency, but the harder the CPU has to work. If you lower the buffer size too much, the setting can produce crackling noises, although this is a function of the horsepower of the computer. These noises crop up when the CPU literally has to drop audio bytes because it can't keep up with the audio stream.

Today's fast computers can get the I/O buffer size down to 64 samples (1.3 ms at a 48k sampling rate) without too much trouble, but the more tracks and processing you add (especially when running at sampling rates higher than 48kHz), the harder the computer's CPU will have to work, which means you may need to increase the buffer size to prevent dropouts.

It should be noted that it's best to NOT use any software plug-in processing like compressors or EQ when recording since each plug-in adds anywhere from a little to a lot of latency just by being inserted in the signal path. Keep that path as efficient as possible with as few things between the mic and the recorder as you can, and your signal will not only sound better but will stay in sync as well.

Many audio interfaces are equipped with zero-latency monitoring, which is an analog bus that loops directly from the interface's input to its output without passing through the computer. Once you've set up this routing in your interface's control panel applet (it comes with the interface), the player or singer will be able to monitor the backing tracks and get his or her performance in sync without any time delay whatsoever.

CHAPTER 4
RECORDING BASICS

While we assume that you have at least a little recording experience if you're reading this book, let's take a brief look at some of the principles in case you're not sure.

The Signal Path

The typical recording signal path goes like this: the sound source (an instrument, vocal, or amplifier) into the microphone, into the microphone preamp (either on a recording console or mixer, or a dedicated unit), into the recorder (see Figure 4.1). Sometimes a compressor and/or an EQ is inserted after the mic preamp as well, but it may not always be needed.

Choosing A Preamp

While just about any good preamp will get the job done, many engineers tend to have a favorite model they turn to for recording certain instruments, either because of the color the preamp conveys,

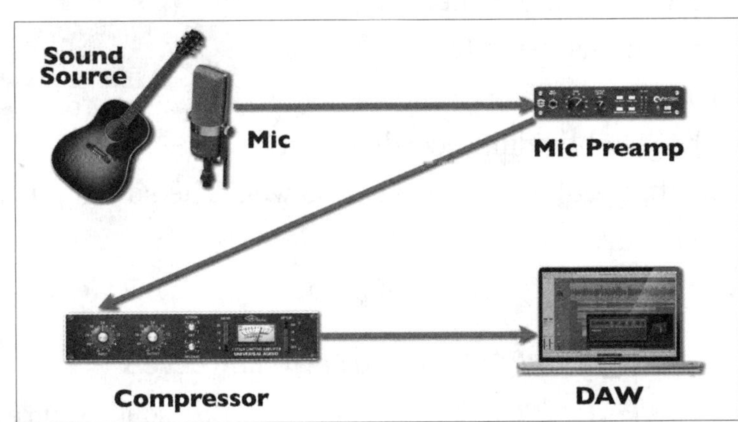

Figure 4.1: A Typical Recording Signal Path

or because a certain mic/preamp combination provides the best sound for the track. Other engineers may choose to combine a good mic with as neutral a preamp as possible, meaning one that does not impart any sonic color of its own on the instrument or vocal.

Since everyone has different ears and opinions, the type of preamp to choose is an open-ended topic, but if you have one that has a "transparent" sound, try that first. If not, try to at least use the highest quality preamp you can, especially on acoustic instruments.

Setting The Recording Level

The meter level reading can sometimes be confusing when recording, so "How high should it be?" is a frequent question. For the most part, you *do not* have to record with the level close to 0 dB (the highest it will go before the red overload indicator lights) these days. In the early days of digital recording, this practice was a necessity in order to keep the noise to a minimum, but modern 24-bit recording no longer has this limitation. If your signal peaks between -6 and -10 dB or even lower on the channel meter, it will sound fine.

Headroom

Headroom means that by recording at a level around -10 dB or so, there's plenty of room left to adequately record short bursts of sound (called transients) without causing any distortion. Sometimes these bursts of energy are so short that an LED overload indicator might not even catch them (like on some of the less expensive equipment available).

These super fast transients make up the first part of the sound of just about any instrument, but especially tambourines, drums, and other percussion. These transients can typically range as high as 20 dB above what an old fashioned VU meter (see Figure 4.2) might indicate (peak meters are much closer to the actual true recording level). Recording too hot means that those transients are trimmed off the signal by overloading the input for less than a millisecond (a thousandth of a second). This results in not only a slightly dull recording, but one that sounds less realistic as well. The solution is to record at a lower level to improve the headroom. By recording at -10 dB or so, you leave plenty of headroom with less of a chance for distorting. Remember that it's easy enough to increase the gain later.

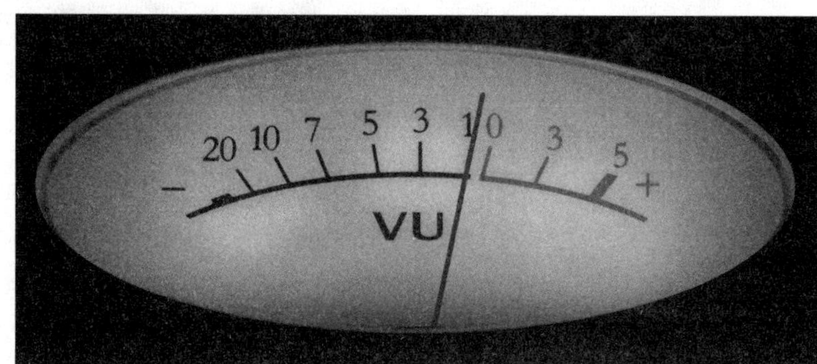

Figure 4.2: An Old Fashioned VU Meter

Exercise Pod: Setting The Recording Levels

E4.1: A) With a microphone set up on a sound source and a microphone preamp set as in E3.1, set the record levels so that they're around -10 dB with peaks about to -6 or so. Does the overload indicator light? Can you hear any distortion? Is the signal clean?

B) Set the record level so that it's as close to 0 dB as you can get. Does the overload indicator light? Can you hear any distortion? Is the signal clean?

C) Set the record level high enough so that the red overload indicator stays lit. Does the sound change at all? Can you hear any distortion?

D) Reset the record levels so that they're around -10 dB with peaks about to -6 or so.

Gain Staging

Gain staging is the proper level setting of each section of the signal path so that none of them overload. On an mixer or console, you're trying to make sure that the input gain doesn't overload the equalizer section, which in turn doesn't overload the panning amplifier, which in turn doesn't overload the fader buffer, which in turn doesn't overload the bus, which doesn't overload the master bus. This is the reason why a pre-fader and after-fader listen (PFL and AFL, or just plain "solo") exist: so you can monitor a different point in the signal path to make sure there's no distortion.

While all of these stages may not be tweakable, one rule exists in the analog world that aptly applies in the digital world as well: the level of any channel faders should always stay below the level of the subgroup or master fader.

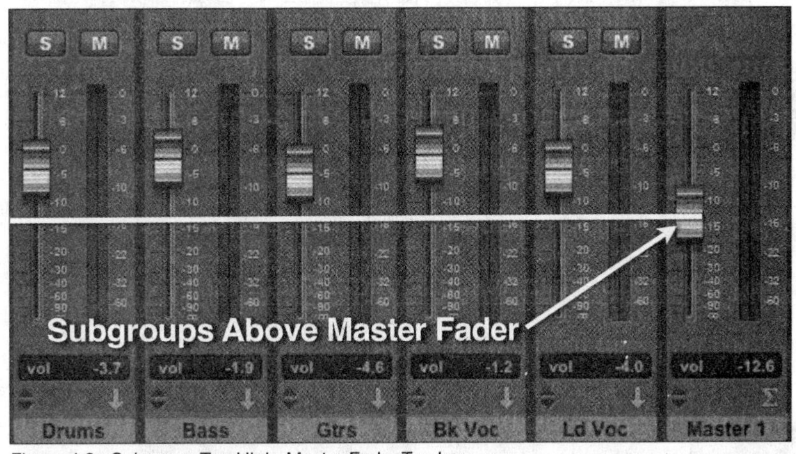

Figure 4.3: Subgroup Too High, Master Fader Too Low

This means that the level of the master fader should always be placed higher than each of the channel faders (see Figure 4.3 and 4.4). While one or two channels might be OK if slightly above, just a single channel with big chunks of EQ (like +10 dB of a frequency band) can lead to anywhere from subtle coloration to outright distortion.

Figure 4.4: Channel and Subgroups Faders At Correct Levels

Exercise Pod: Proper Gain Staging

E4.2: A) Using an audio signal as set up in E4.1, set the input fader on the console or DAW at 0 dB and the master fader to 0 dB. Do the master meter overload indicators light? Can you hear any distortion? Is the signal clean?

B) Set the master fader to -30 dB and increase the monitor level so it's about the same level as in A. Can you hear any difference in the sound? Can you hear any distortion? Is the signal clean? Is it noisy?

DI Setup

Not much setup is required to use a direct box. For the most part, you just plug the instrument in and play. About the only thing that you might have to set is the gain (which is usually only a switch that provides a 10 dB boost or so) on an active box or the ground switch. Most DIs have a ground switch to reduce hum in the event of a ground loop between the instrument and the DI. Set it to the quietest position.

If It's Distorting

If something sounds distorted, use the following steps to track it down:

- Is the microphone preamp overloading? Does the red overload LED light or is the meter peaking into the red? If so, decrease the input gain, or select the input pad or the pad on the mic, if it has one.

- Is your signal path overloading in another place? If you're using a console (regardless of the size) or an outboard compressor, check to see if any overload LEDs are lighting and if the meters are peaking into the red. If so, decrease the output level of the stage before the overload.

- Is your DAW overloading? Once again, check to be sure that no overload LEDs are lit. This shouldn't happen if you keep your input level between -6 and -10 dB. If it does, decrease the input level on the DAW, or the output level of the previous gain stage.

- Is your playback signal path distorting? Are you listening back through a console? If so, is one of those channels overloading? Are the monitors turned up too loud? Are there any overload lights lit anywhere in the signal path? If so, decrease the level from the DAW first, or turn down any input level controls in the playback signal path.

- Is it a mic or cable? Replace the cable first. Is the sound cleaner? If not, try a different mic. Any better?

- Is it a cabinet rattle? Sometimes a recording picks up something that you can't hear live unless you really look for it. For instance, a buzz coming from a loose amp handle can sometimes be interpreted as distortion. Go out into the room and listen to the instrument and the environment closely, but be sure to have the player play the exact same part as when you heard the distortion. Sometimes the sound will only come from a single note, so by playing the same part you ensure that it can happen again so you can track it down.

Compression Basics

A compressor is used during recording usually because the dynamics of the instrument that you're trying to record are out of control. This means that some notes may be getting lost because they're too low, or the peaks may be too high and threatening to overload.

As a result, compression tries to keep the level of the sound even by lifting the level of the soft passages and lowering the level of the loud ones so that there's less of a difference between them. This is typically accomplished by compressing anywhere from 2 to 6 dB or so at anywhere from a 2:1 to 12:1 ratio, although some situations may require more radical settings.

Using The Compressor

Usually the *Input* or *Threshold* control will set the amount of compression occurring while the *Output* or *Make-Up Gain* control will control the output level. The *Ratio* control will also have a part in controlling the amount of compression that occurs. The timing of the *Attack* and *Release* is important, so here are a few steps to set up the compressor. *The idea is to make the compressor breathe in time with the song.*

Exercise Pod: Setting Up The Compressor

E4.3: A) Using the audio signal that you set up in E4.1, set the microphone up and insert the compressor into the signal chain, then slowly decrease the *Threshold* until the *Gain Reduction Meter* reads 2 dB. Can you hear the compression? What does the input meter of the DAW read? Can you hear a difference if you bypass the compressor?

B) Increase the *Threshold* until the *Gain Reduction Meter* reads 10 dB. Can you hear the compression? What does the input meter of the DAW read? Can you hear a difference if you bypass the compressor?

C) Return the *Threshold* control to where there's only 2 dB of gain reduction. Now increase the *Ratio* control from 2:1 to 6:1. What does the gain reduction meter read now? What does the input meter of the DAW read? Can you hear the compression? Can you hear a difference if you bypass the compressor?

D) Now increase the *Ratio* control from 2:1 to 20:1. What does the gain reduction meter read now? What does the input meter of the DAW read? Can you hear the compression? Can you hear the difference if you bypass the compressor?

E) Return the *Ratio* control to 4:1 and increase the *Threshold* control until there's about 3 dB of gain reduction occurring. Now decrease the *Attack* time to as fast as it will go. What does the gain reduction meter read now? What does the input meter of the DAW read? Can you hear the compression? Can you hear the difference if you bypass the compressor?

F) Increase the *Attack* time to as slow as it will go. What does the gain reduction meter read now? What does the input meter of the DAW read? Can you hear the compression? Can you hear the difference if you bypass the compressor?

G) Now decrease the *Attack* time until the sound of the instrument just begins to dull. What does the gain reduction meter read now? What does the input meter of the DAW read? Can you hear the compression? Can you hear the difference if you bypass the compressor?

H) Increase the *Release* time to as slow as it will go. What does the gain reduction meter read now? What does the input meter of the DAW read? Can you hear the compression? Can you hear the difference if you bypass the compressor?

I) Decrease the *Release* time to as fast as it will go. What does the gain reduction meter read now? What does the input meter of the DAW read? Can you hear the compression? Can you hear the difference if you bypass the compressor?

J) Increase the *Release* time so it bounces with the pulse of the song. What does the gain reduction meter read now? What does the input meter of the DAW read? Can you hear the compression? Can you hear the difference if you bypass the compressor?

K) Select the *Bypass* to hear the volume of the sound without the compressor. Now deselect the *Bypass* and slowly raise the *Output* control until the compressed signal level is equal to the uncompressed signal in level. Continue to use the *Bypass* to check.

L) Set the controls to a small bit of limiting (2 or 3 dB) to keep from overloading on the loud sections of the recording.

How Much Compression Do I Need?

How much compression you use is a matter of taste. That being said, the more compression you use, the more likely that you'll hear it working. Generally speaking, compression of 6 dB or less is used more for controlling dynamics than for imparting any sonic quality, but it's also common to see as much as 15 or even 20 dB used for room mics and sometimes even vocals, depending upon the situation. In the final analysis, the amount of compression depends on the song, the arrangement, the player, the room, the instrument or vocalist, or the sound you're looking for.

Limiting

As said before, a compressor and a limiter are the same except for the settings. Any time the compression ratio is set to 10:1 or more, it's considered a limiter. Limiting during recording is usually used to tame some of the uncontrolled peaks of a sound that might be causing distortion.

Many times during recording it's better to use limiting instead of compression since you're trying to keep the signal from overloading instead of trying to even out its dynamic range or change the sound. As a result, massive amounts of limiting aren't used that much, with only a few dB being the norm.

Equalization Basics

Before you begin twisting equalizer knobs, it helps to understand the situations where EQing might be helpful, since there's more than one. They are:

- To make an instrument sound clearer and more defined.

- To make the instrument sound bigger and larger than life.

- To make all the elements of a mix fit better together.

It's all too common for someone new to recording to solo a track, grab the EQ, and endlessly search for what seems to be the right sound. The only problem is that sometimes the right sound can be found faster and easier by just moving a microphone a little instead. Remember, there's no rule that says you have to use the EQ at all if the track sounds good and works with the other tracks already.

Using The Equalizer

In Chapter 3 we looked at the subtractive equalization method of EQing, which, while not the only method, is always a good place to start. There are two frequency ranges that are particularly effective when using subtractive equalization; between 200 to 600Hz and between 2k and 4kHz. The reason why 200 to 600Hz is chosen is because most directional microphones provide a natural low frequency boost because of the proximity effect brought about by miking an instrument or voice up close, but that area in particular makes everything sound cloudy. Likewise, many mics that are known as good vocal mics have a presence boost between 2k and 4kHz. Cutting those frequencies a few dB (more or less as needed) can make the track sound much more natural than if you were to try to boost other frequencies instead.

These two problem areas usually crop up when you're recording everything with the same microphone, since there's a buildup in the those frequency areas as more and more instruments are recorded. By cutting a few dB from these frequency ranges, you'll find that the instruments sit better in the mix without ever having to add much EQ.

Exercise Pod: Using The Equalizer

E4.4: Using The EQ

A) Using the audio signal that you set up in E4.1, set the *Boost/Cut* control to a moderate level of cut (8 or 10 dB should work.)

B) Sweep through the frequencies until you find the frequency where the sound has the least amount of boxiness and the most definition.

C) Adjust the amount of cut to taste.

D) Now set the *Boost/Cut* control to a moderate level of *boost* (8 or 10 dB should work.)

E) Sweep through the frequencies until you find the frequency where the sound jumps out. Stay on this frequency.

F) Decrease the boost to 0 db, then cut 2 dB at that frequency. Does the sound seem more natural? Does the sound seem to have more low end? Does it seem to have more high end?

G) Now cut 4 dB at that frequency. Does the sound seem more natural? Does the sound seem to have more low end? Does it seem to have more high end?

H) Now cut 6 dB at that frequency. Does the sound seem more natural? Does the sound seem to have more low end? Does it seem to have more high end? Does it now seem to be missing something?

I) Set the amount of cut to where the sound has the most definition.

The Magic High-Pass Filter

One of the most useful and overlooked equalization parameters available is the high-pass filter (HPF). The high-pass filter can be another parameter on an equalizer, or it can be a stand-alone plug-in or device. The HPF does just what it says—it allows high frequencies to pass and cuts off low frequencies.

The low frequencies of many instruments sometimes just clash with each other and, in the end, don't add much to the sound anyway. That's why if you roll the low frequencies off below 100Hz on most instruments other than the kick and bass, the mix begins to clean up almost magically.

For instance, by rolling off the low frequencies of a vocal mic, you can eliminate the rumble of trucks and machinery that you can't physically hear because they're so low, yet muddy up the mix. Rolling off the low end of an electric guitar keeps it out of the way of the rhythm section and helps it to fit better in the mix. Even rolling off the bass or drums anywhere between 40 and 60Hz can sometimes make the mix both louder and punchier without any sense of losing the low end.

Exercise Pod: Using The High-Pass Filter

E4.5: A) Using the audio signal that you set up in E4.1, insert a HPF at 60Hz. Is the sound cleaner? Does it sound different from before? Does it lack bottom?

B) Increase the frequency of the HPF to 80Hz. Is the sound cleaner? Does it sound different from before? Does it lack bottom?

C) Increase the frequency of the HPF to 100Hz. Is the sound cleaner? Does it sound different from before? Does it lack bottom?

D) Increase the frequency of the HPF to 200Hz. Is the sound cleaner? Does it sound different from before? Does it lack bottom?

E) Set the HPF to where it doesn't interfere with low frequencies of the sound source or it fits better with the bass and drums.

The Principles of Equalization

Here are some general equalization principles that can speed up the EQ process and keep you from chasing your EQ tail.

- If it sounds muddy, cut some at 250Hz.

- If it sounds honky, cut some at 500Hz.

- Cut if you're trying to make things sound clearer.

- Boost if you're trying to make things sound different.

- You can't boost something that's not there in the first place.

CHAPTER 5
MICROPHONE PLACEMENT BASICS

Before we can begin placing microphones, it's extremely helpful to learn the basics of what to listen for. While many engineers have learned just by emulating other engineers (which isn't a bad thing as long as you emulate the right person), it really pays to learn some of the behind-the-scenes skills. That way, whenever something out of the ordinary pops up, you'll easily know how to handle it.

Microphone Technique 101

Before we get into the nitty gritty of actual microphone placement, there are a number of issues that are many times overlooked. Regardless of what instrument you're recording, here are a few things to consider first.

Choosing The Best Place In The Room

The room itself can make a big difference in the sound of an instrument, which is why it's best to find the place in the room that's acoustically beneficial to the sound. When you're tracking with a group of players (especially a rhythm section), finding the best placement in the room is secondary to leakage concerns and player sight lines, but during overdubs, finding the most complementary place in the room is crucial.

What you're looking for is a spot where the instrument sounds relatively live without the environment acting as a detriment to the sound. Try these following steps to find the best room placement:

- **Test the room by walking around and clapping your hands.** That's a good way to find a place in the room that has a nice even reverb decay. If the clap has a "boing" to it (a funny sounding repeated overtone), so will the sound of the instrument, so it's best to try another place in the room where it will hopefully sound smoother. If you can't find a place without a boing, place the instrument where it sounds the smoothest and try putting some padding or something soft (as discussed in Chapter 1) on one of the side walls to break up any standing waves.

- **It's usually best to stay out of a corner.** The corner normally causes "bass loading," meaning that the low frequencies will be reinforced causing some low notes to boom. For instance, when you're tracking this can lead to sympathetic tom ringing and snare buzzing on the drum kit.

- **Ideally, you don't want to be too close to a wall.** The reflections (or absorption if the wall is soft) can change the sound of the instrument, especially if it's very loud and omnidirectional, like drums or percussion. The middle of the room usually works best.

- **Ideally, you want to be at the place in the room where the ceiling height is the highest.** If the ceiling is vaulted, try placing the instrument in the middle of the vault first, then move it as needed.

- **Stay away from glass if you can.** Glass will give you a lot of unwanted reflections that will change the sound of the instrument. If you have no choice because of the way the room is designed or the players are situated, try setting the instrument up at a 45° angle to the glass (see Figure 5.1).

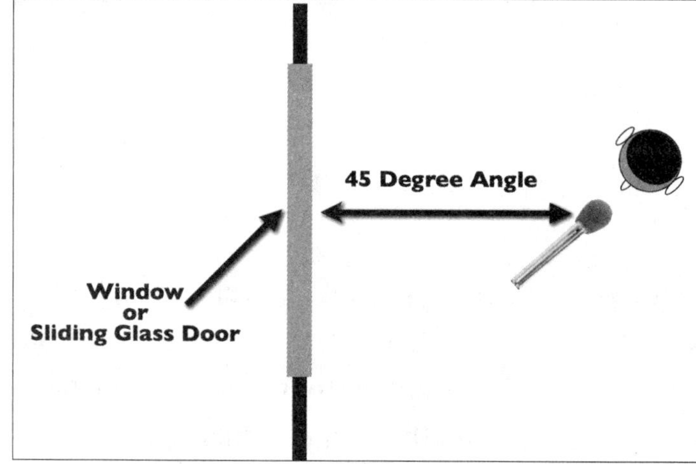

Figure 5.1: Set The Player To A 45° Angle To Any Glass

- **Try putting a rug under the vocal or instrument.** A rug stops any reflections off the floor that can sometimes have a negative impact on the overall sound. On the other hand, sometimes the reflections from a hard floor can enhance the sound. Try it both ways and choose.

- **For an amplifier, try placing it on a chair or road case.** When the amp is decoupled from the floor, there are fewer phase cancellations on the low end, so the sound will be more direct and distinct. Acoustic foam like Auralex placed underneath the amp also works as well.

Exercise Pod: Microphone Placement 101

E5.1: Finding The Best Place In The Room

A) Walk around the room while clapping your hands. Does the room ring? How long is the decay? Can you hear it "boing"? Is there a place that the decay sounds especially smooth? Place the instrument there.

B) Walk into a corner while clapping your hands. How long is the decay? Can you hear it "boing"? Does it sound better or worse than in the middle of the room?

C) Place the instrument, amplifier, or singer in a corner. Is there more or less bass than in the middle of the room? Does it sound better or worse there?

D) Place the instrument, amplifier, or singer right next to a wall. Is there more or less bass than in the middle of the room? Does it sound better or worse there?

E) Place a rug underneath the instrument, amplifier, or singer. Is there more or less bass? Are there more or fewer reflections? Does it sound better or worse?

F) If miking an amplifier, place it on the floor first. Note the sound. Now place a rug underneath. Is there more or less bass? Are there more or fewer reflections? Does it sound better or worse? Now place it on a chair or road case. Is there more or less bass? Are there more or fewer reflections? Does it sound better or worse?

Choosing The Right Mic

The microphone choice should be made so it complements the sound of the instrument or amplifier if you want the recording to sound smooth with no peaks in the response. If you have several mics to choose from, go through this list before you make your choice.

- **There's no single mic that works on everything.** Just because you have a great mic doesn't necessarily mean that it will be the best choice in all situations. Also see the third point in this list.

- **Choose the mic for the right reasons.** Just because a mic is considered an industry "standard" choice for a particular application doesn't necessarily mean that it'll work in your situation. Likewise, just because your favorite engineer, player, or singer uses a particular mic doesn't mean it will also work for you. There are so many variables that you can never count on anything other than your ears.

- **Select a microphone that complements the instrument or amp.** If the sound of the instrument, vocal, or amplifier is edgy or has a lot of top end, you wouldn't want to choose a mic that emphasizes that frequency range since it will sound even more out-of-balance frequency-wise. On the other hand, a mic that emphasizes the upper midrange a bit might make a mellower sounding instrument step out of the mix. Choose the mic to help overcome some of the deficiencies of the sound of the instrument.

- **Consider the pickup pattern of the mic.** A directional mic is not always the best choice for the sound you're trying to capture. When you're not worried about leakage (during overdubs, for instance), an omni or figure 8 pattern might provide a smoother sound with better sounding ambiance (providing you're recording in a good sounding room).

- **Consider the proximity effect.** The closer a directional mic gets to the sound source, the more the bass response increases. This isn't always desirable, so either move the mic back from the source a bit, or change the pattern to omni. On the other hand, you can also use proximity effect to your advantage to increase the low end of a sound if needed.

- **Large diaphragm condensers are not necessarily better than small diaphragm condensers.** Contrary to popular belief, small diaphragm condenser microphones can reproduce the lower frequencies better (if that's what you're after), and are generally less colored off-axis than large diaphragm mics. Large diaphragm mics aren't as noisy though.

E5.2: Choosing The Right Mic

A) Listen to the sound of the instrument or vocal in the tracking room. Is it big and boomy? Is it thin and nasal sounding? Is there a frequency range that sticks out?

B) Choose a mic that has an opposite color of the voice or instrument. If it's thin and bright, choose a dynamic or ribbon mic. If it's dull and bassy, try a condenser. What does it sound like? Does the mic complement the instrument? Are there any frequency areas that stick out?

C) Choose a mic that has the same color of the voice or instrument. If it's thin and bright, choose a condenser mic. If it's dull and bassy, try a dynamic or ribbon. Does the mic complement the instrument? What does it sound like? Are there any frequency areas that stick out?

D) Try using a cardioid mic. What is the bass response like? What is the treble response like? Is there any leakage? Does the leakage sound clear or muffled?

E) Switch to an omnidirectional mic. What happened to the bass response? What happened to the treble response? Is there any leakage? Does the leakage sound clear or muffled?

F) Switch to a figure eight mic. What happened to the bass response? What happened to the treble response? Is there any leakage? Does the leakage sound clear or muffled?

The Secret To Mic Placement

A common recording process has an engineer EQing, compressing, and adding multiple mics when trying to record an instrument, all the while never taking into account what the sound in the room at the source is like. That's why it's important to use the following steps in any serious microphone placement before reaching for the EQ or any signal processing:

1. **Go out into the room, stand in front of the instrument, and listen to the musician play the part from the song you're about to record.** Playing the song is important because you might be deceived if it's another song or just random playing. Listen for the tonal balance from the vocal, amp, or instrument as well as the way the room responds to it. Listening to the instrument in the room will give you a reference point to the way it really sounds so you can compare it to what you hear in the speakers in the control room.

2. **Find the sweet spot.** There are several ways to find the sweet spot.

- To place an omnidirectional mic, cover one ear and listen with the other. Move around player until you find the spot that sounds best. That's where to place the mic as a starting point.

- To place a cardioid mic, cup your hand behind your ear (instead of covering it) and move around the player or amp until you find the place that sounds best. That's where to place the mic as a starting point.

- To place a stereo mic or stereo pair, cup both ears and move around the player or amp until you find the place that sounds best. That's where to place the mic as a starting point.

3. **You can't place the mic by sight.** The best mic position must always be found, not predicted. It's okay to have a starting place, but may not be what ends up being the best spot.

4. **Change the mic position instead of reaching for the EQ.** Chances are that you can adjust the quality of the sound enough by simply moving the mic in order to avoid using any equalization. The EQ is difficult to undo later and can inflict some unwanted electronic artifacts that can never be removed. Moving the mic (which is really acoustic equalization when it comes down to it) will usually sound smoother and more pleasing to the ear.

5. **Give the mic some distance.** Remember, *distance creates depth*. The guitar and amp will sound a lot more natural than using artificial ambiance. If possible, leave just enough distance between the mic and the source to get a bit of room reflection to it.

E5.3: Microphone Placement

A) Stand next to the player and listen while he plays the song you're about to record. What does the instrument sound like? Is it big and boomy? Is it thin and nasal sounding? Is there a frequency range that sticks out?

B) After you've chosen a mic as illustrated by E5.2, walk around the instrument until you find the spot where it sounds the most balanced frequency-wise. Place the mic there. How does the sound interact with the room? Is there a spot where it sounds better? What does it sound like when you cup your hand behind your ear?

C) After listen to the sound over the monitors, move the mic six inches to the right. Has the sound changed? Is there more or less high end? Is there more or less low end?

D) What happens when you move the mic six inches to the left? Has the sound changed? Is there more or less high end? Is there more or less low end? What happens if you move it in between?

E) After you've found the spot that sounds the best, move the mic back six inches. Can you hear more of the room? Does it sound better or worse?

F) Now move it back a foot beyond that. Can you hear more of the room? Does it sound better or worse? Return it to its original position.

G) Now move the mic in three inches. Can you hear more or less of the room? Does it sound better or worse? Is there more low end? Move it back six inches beyond that. Can you hear more or less of the room? Does it sound better or worse? Is there more low end?

H) Place the mic were you have the best balance of low, mid, and high frequencies, and the best balance of direct to ambient sound.

Phase Cancellation: The Sound Destroyer

Throughout the book we'll constantly refer to a phenomenon known as "phase cancellation," and with good reason. One of the most important and overlooked aspects of recording is to make sure that the mics are all in-phase if more than one is used at the same time. The reason is because with just a single out-of-phase mic, a multi-miked instrument like a drum kit will never sound right, and if not corrected, may never be able to be fixed.

So just what is phase anyway? Without getting into an intense technical explanation, it just means that the output from all the microphones used on the session are pushing and pulling together as one. If one mic is pushing while another is pulling, they cancel each other out at certain frequencies. In Figure 5.2, when mic No. 1's signal peaks, mic No. 2's signal valleys. They cancel each other out at that frequency and the result is a very weak-sounding signal when mixed together.

In Figure 5.3, both mics are pushing and pulling together. Their signal peaks happen at the same time as do their valleys. As a result, their signals reinforce one another.

Acoustic Phase Cancellation

There are two types of phase cancellation problems that can happen: electronic and acoustic. An acoustic phasing problem occurs when two mics are too close together and pick up the sound from the same instrument, except one is picking it up a little later than the first because it's farther away (see Figure 5.4).

With acoustic phase problems, the sounds won't cancel each other out completely, only at certain frequencies. This usually makes the sound of the two mixed together sound either hollow or just lack depth and bottom end.

The way to eliminate the problem is by moving mic No. 2 a little further away from mic No. 1, or if the mics are directional, making sure that each one is pointing directly at the source they're trying to capture.

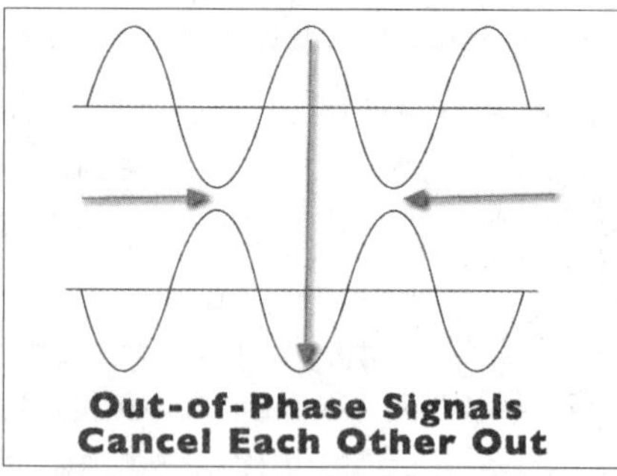

Figure 5.2: Two Microphones Out-Of-Phase

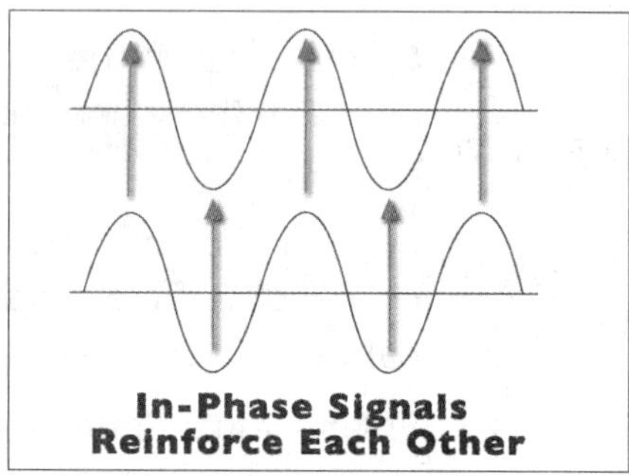

Figure 5.3: Two Microphones In-Phase

The 3 To 1 Principle

The 3 to 1 Principle states that in order to avoid phase cancellation between microphones, a second mic should never be within three times the distance that the first mic is from its source. For instance, if a pair of microphones were placed over the sound board of a piano at a distance of 1 foot, the separation between the two mics should be at least 3 feet. If the distance from the source was 2 feet, the distance between mics should be at least 6 feet (see Figure 5.5).

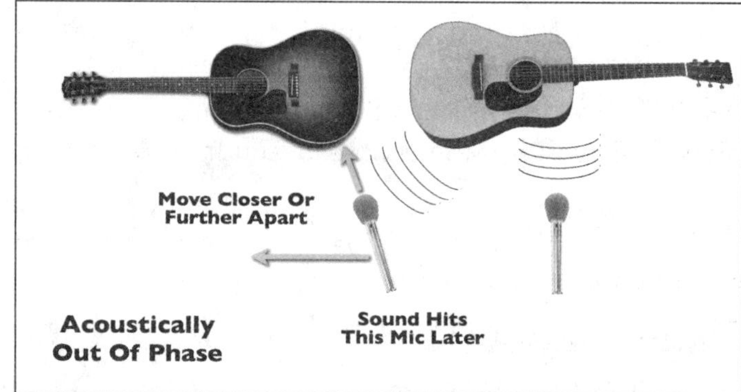

Figure 5.4: Acoustically Out Of Phase

This principle is not a hard and fast rule, but it certainly is a good guideline for eliminating phase problems. Remember, if you record something with a phase problem, no amount of EQ or processing can ever make it right afterwards.

Electronic Phase Cancellation

While we'll mostly be talking about acoustic phase problems in the book, there's also an instance of electronic phase cancellation that you should know about as well. This has nothing to do with mic placement as it's strictly an electronic problem that never shows up until multiple mics are used.

Electronic phase problems are almost always caused by a cable in the studio (usually a mic cable) that's been mis-wired during an install, repaired incorrectly, or originally wired incorrectly from the factory (which is rare). There are two ways to check the electronic phase without using an electronic test device.

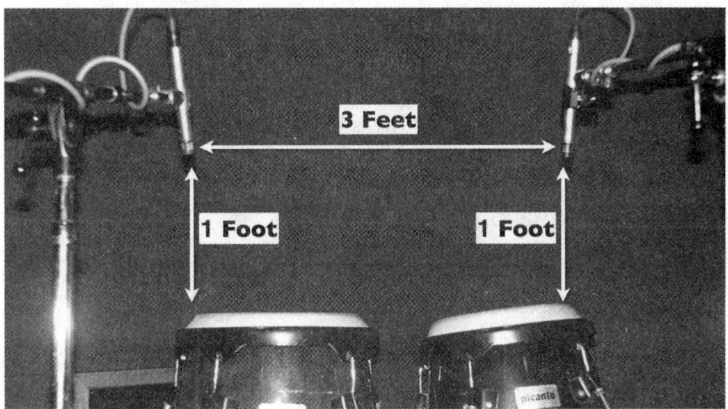

Figure 5.5: The 3 To 1 Principle

Checking Phase

Checking microphone phase is one of the first things to do after the mics are wired up and tested. This is especially the case in a tracking session in which a lot of mics will be used, since having just one mic out of phase can cause uncorrectable sonic problems that will haunt the recording forever. A session that is in-phase will sound bigger and punchier while just a single out-of-phase mic will make the entire mix sound tiny and weak.

If you're going to be absolutely thorough, there are actually two tests: one for polarity and one for phase. The polarity check is used mainly to be sure that all mics are pushing and pulling the same way and

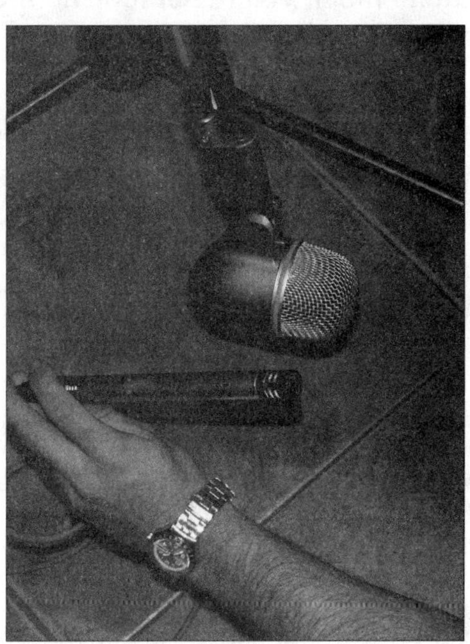
Figure 5.6: Checking Polarity

to check for mis-wired cables (yes, they're out there, especially if you build your own). The phase check will ensure that you minimize the interference between the mics when they're placed.

Remember that the *Phase Switch* on the mic preamp, DAW interface, or console is really a polarity switch, which changes the phase by 180 degrees at all frequencies by swapping pins 2 and 3 of a balanced microphone line. It may get the problem frequencies closer to being in phase, or it may get them further away. It depends on what the problems are, and the placement of the mics.

Exercise Pod: Checking Phase

E5.4: Checking Polarity

A) After the mics are set up, wired, and checked, but not necessarily placed, pick one mic that can be easily moved. This can be a scratch vocal mic, a hat mic, or guitar mic; it doesn't matter as long as it works, sounds good to begin with (it's not defective), and can move next to the farthest mic used in the session. This mic will become our reference mic.

B) With the reference mic in hand, move it next to the kick drum mic (or any other mic that you wish to test for that matter). Put both mics together so the capsules touch and speak into them from about a foot away (the distance isn't critical—see Figure 5.6).

C) Bring up the faders on both mics so the audio level (not the fader position) is equal on both.

D) Flip the phase of the mic under test (in this case, the kick mic). Does one position have more low end than another? Choose the position that gives you the most low end.

E) Repeat for all the other mics.

Remember, you're not flipping the phase of the reference mic, only the mic that you're testing.

Checking Phase By Listening

Checking the phase is essential not only on the drums but any instrument being miked with more than a single microphone. That said, the chances for a phase problem are far greater on the drum kit since it usually has more mics on it than any other instrument. The mics will never be completely in-phase, but some problems will be diminished by reversing polarity on some of the channels. The only way to determine this is through experimentation and listening. Here's a way to check the *phase* after the drums have been recorded.

E5.5: Checking The Phase By Listening

A) Listen to the overheads on your monitors with them panned hard left and right, then listen to them panned to the center. Do they sound thin or swishy when they're panned in the center? Is there more low end when you flip the phase switch on one of them? Choose the position of the phase switch that sounds the best, pan them back into stereo, then go on to the next step.

B) Add the kick drum channel to the mix. Switch the polarity on the kick channel of the console or DAW. Is there more low end when you flip the phase switch? Stay with the position that has the fullest sound.

C) Add the snare drum channel to the mix. Switch the polarity on the snare channel of the console or DAW. Is there more low end when you flip the phase switch? Stay with the position that has the fullest sound.

D) Do this for each channel that's been recorded. Always stay with the position of the phase switch that has the most bottom.

Ultimately, you can't totally avoid phase cancellation, but you can make sure that it sounds as good as possible.

Remember: one position of the phase switch will always sounds fuller than the other.

CHAPTER 6
RECORDING THE DRUMS

If there's one instrument that producers and engineers alike seem to obsess over, it's the drum kit. And well they should, since drums are the heartbeat of virtually all modern music. Wimpy sounding drums make a recording sound wimpy regardless of how well everything else is recorded.

The problem is that most drummers' kits simply don't record well either because they're using old beat up heads (the worst offender), are tuned badly, or have defective hardware. As a result, drums that might be adequate or even great sounding in a live situation don't always make the cut when put under the microscope of the recording studio.

Many producers and engineers are willing to spend whatever time it takes to make the drums sound great in the room, because if the drum sound there doesn't cut it, then there's not much the engineer can do to help (despite what the makers of outboard gear and plug-ins might tell you). But just what constitutes a great sounding drum kit?

The Keys To A Great Sounding Drum Kit

While the definition of great is different to different people, in the studio it usually means *a kit that's free of buzzes and sympathetic vibrations*. This means that when you hit the a rack tom, the snare drum doesn't buzz and the other toms don't ring along with it, and if you hit the snare, the toms don't ring along. So how do you achieve this drum nirvana? It's all in the tuning and the kit maintenance.

The Tuning Technique

Most engineers (and even a lot of drummers) don't know the proper way to tune their drums, but it's not a difficult process. For a drum to be properly tuned, you've got to keep all of the tension rods that hold the head on even so they have the same tension at each lug. What you want is for the pitch to sound the same at each lug as you tap near it.

Exercise Pod: Tuning The Drums

E6.1: Tuning The Drums

A) Hit the head an inch in front of each lug of the drum. Is the sound the same at each lug?

B) Using a drum key, adjust the tension so that the sound is the same at each lug. Is the sound the same at each lug now?

C) When the pitch (the tension) is the same at each lug, hitting the drum in the center should result in a nice, even decay.

D) Using the same technique, tune the the bottom head to the same pitch as the top head. What does the drum sound like now when you hit it in the center? Is the tone even? Is the decay even? Are there any overtones?

E) Using the same technique, try to tune the bottom head down a 3rd to a 5th below the top head. What does the drum sound like now when you hit it in the center? Is the tone even? Is the decay even? Are there any overtones?

Tuning Tips And Tricks

Here are some tuning tips and tricks from Ross Garfield, the famous Drum Doctor (check him out at drumdoctors.com).

Snare Tuning Tips

The snare is probably the most important drum in the kit because you hear it on at least every beat 2 and 4. That's why it's important to get the snare tuned first.

If the snare drum has too much ring:

- Tune the heads lower.

- Use a heavier head like a coated Remo Emperor.

- Use a full or partial muffling ring (you can also add some tape or Moongel).

If the snare drum doesn't have enough ring:

- Tune the head higher.

- Use a thinner head like a coated Remo Ambassador or Diplomat.

If the snares buzz when the tom-toms are hit:

- Check that the snares (the curled wires on the bottom of the drum) are straight. Replace as needed.

- Check that the snares are flat and centered on the drum.

- Loosen the bottom head.

- Retune the offending toms.

- Use an alternate snare drum.

Kick Drum Tuning Tips

If the kick drum isn't punchy and lacks power when played in the context of the music, you can try the following:

- Try increasing and decreasing the amount of muffling in the drum.

- Change to a heavier, uncoated head like a clear Remo Emperor or PowerStroke 3.

- Change to a thinner front head or one with a larger cutout.

Tom Tuning Tips

The kick and snare are the two most important drums, so most drummers tune the toms around them to try to make sure that the rack toms aren't being set off when the snare is hit. Try to tune the toms so that the smallest have the shortest decay with the decay getting longer as the drums get bigger. Try to tune each tom as far apart as the song will permit. It's easy to get the right spread between a 13 and a 16 inch tom, but it's more difficult to get it between a 12 and a 13. What I try to do is to tune the 12 up and the 13 down a little.

If one or more of the tom-toms are difficult to tune, don't blend together, or have an unwanted "growl," try the following:

- Check the top heads for dents and replace as necessary.

- Check the evenness of tension all around on the top and bottom heads.

- Tighten the bottom head.

If the floor tom has an undesirable "basketball-type" ring, try this:

- Loosen the bottom head.

- Check the top heads for dents and replace as necessary.

- Loosen the top head.

- Switch to a different type or weight top or bottom head, like a clear Ambassador or Emperor.

Cymbals Tips

Be careful with mixing different cymbal weights when you're recording because of the different volumes that each will have. For example, if you use a couple of thick cymbals, a thinner cymbal might disappear in the mix because it's not as loud. Thicker cymbals are made with a live situation in mind for times when they need to be loud to cut through the band, but they can sound a little gong-like when recording. They can still work for recording if they're all the same weight.

Miking The Individual Drums

There are numerous ways to mike the drums, but what you'll see here is probably the most common approach. You can find a ton of alternative miking techniques in *The Recording Engineer's Handbook*. In the meantime, if your drums sound good in the room already, this method will get you a pretty darn good sounding recording.

Miking The Bass Drum

The bass drum anchors the band and, along with the snare, provides the pulse of the song. Because it can come in different sizes and be used with the front head on or off, its sound will vary a lot more than the other drums.

Most of the time you'll get the best sound out of a bass drum for recording if the front head is removed, since this gets rid on any overtones that the combination of the front and rear head might produce. Even with a hole in the front head, some overtones may still exist. Either way, it's best to place a packing blanket or some heavy towels inside so they just touch both heads to make the sound tight and punchy. Pack the blanket closer to the rear head for more muffling (see Figure 6.1).

The exceptions to this might be in a jazz or classical situation where the drummer just needs to feel the tension that the front head provides in order to play well. If that's the case, you can still get a great sound, as evidenced by the giant drum sounds that John Bonham got on all those Led Zeppelin records.

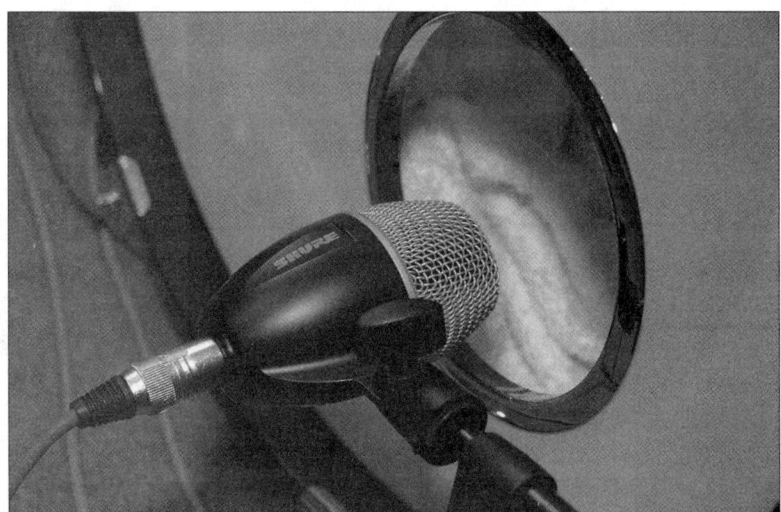

Figure 6.1: Using A Packing Blanket To Muffle The Overtones

A large diaphragm dynamic mic like an AKG D-112, Shure B52, E/V RE20 or 320, or Heil PR 40 is typically used in order to obtain the girth in the kick sound that most modern records require, but don't be afraid to try other microphones as well. The exception is a ribbon mic, since the blast of air coming off the bass drum head can actually be enough to blow the diaphragm out, so it's best to use it on another instrument instead.

Exercise Pod: Miking The Individual Drums

E6.2: Bass Drum Mic Positioning

A) For a kick drum without a front head, place the mic on a short boom stand in front of the bass drum and position the head element of the mic just inside the drum by a couple of inches.

B) Point the mic towards the center of the bass drum, about 8–12" away from the inside head, at about the same height as where the beater hits the drum (see Figure 6.2). Listen on the monitors. Does the drum sound tight and punchy? Does it have enough low end? Can you hear the beater? Are there a lot of overtones? Is there a decay after the drum is hit or does it stop abruptly?

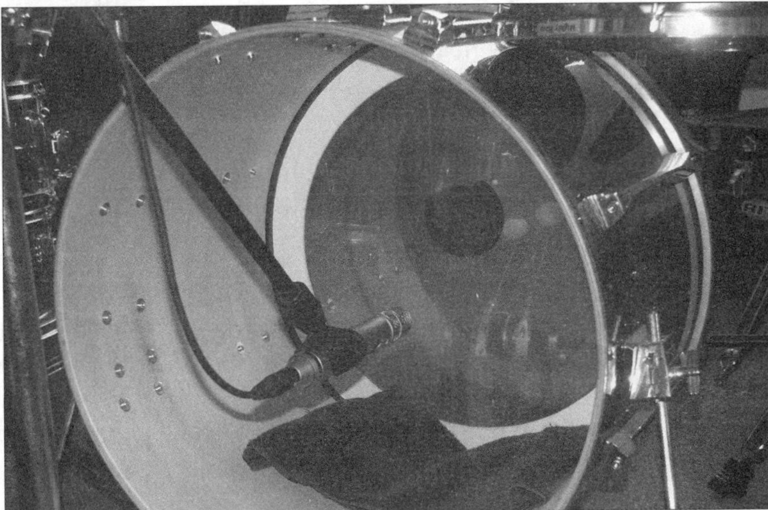

Figure 6.2: Starting Mic Position For Bass Drum With No Front Head

C) To get a tighter, more compact bass drum sound, place a folded packing blanket or a pillow on the inside of the bottom of the drum shell lightly touching the head (see Figure 6.3). Secure it with a weight or even a brick on the blanket to keep it from slipping once you've positioned it to get the perfect sound. Listen on the monitors. Does the drum sound tight and punchy? Does it have enough low end? Can you hear the beater? Are there a lot of overtones? Is there a decay after the drum is hit or does it stop abruptly?

Figure 6.3: Using A Pillow For A Tighter Sound

D) Place the mic where you have the best combination of low end and definition.

E6.3: Miking A Bass Drum With A Front Head

A) Place the mic on a short stand 4 to 6 inches away from the head, halfway up and slightly off-center (see Figure 6.4). Listen on the monitors. Does the drum sound tight and punchy? Does it have enough low end? Can you hear the beater? Are there a lot of overtones? Is there a decay after the drum is hit or does it stop abruptly?

Figure 6.4: Miking A Bass Drum With A Front Head

B) Move the mic away about six inches further away from the head. Listen on the monitors. Does the drum sound have more low end?

C) Move it way about a foot further. Is there more or less low end?

D) Place it where you have the best combination of low end and definition.

E6.4: Miking A Bass Drum With A Front Head With A Hole

A) Place the mic just inside the hole (see Figure 6.5), pointed at where the beater strikes the back head. Listen on the monitors. Does the drum sound tight and punchy? Does it have enough low end? Can you hear the beater? Are there a lot of overtones? Is there a decay after the drum is hit or does it stop abruptly?

B) Aim the mic away from the beater and more at the shell of the drum. Has the sound changed? Can you hear more or less beater? Is there more or less low end?

D) Place it where you have the best combination of low end and definition.

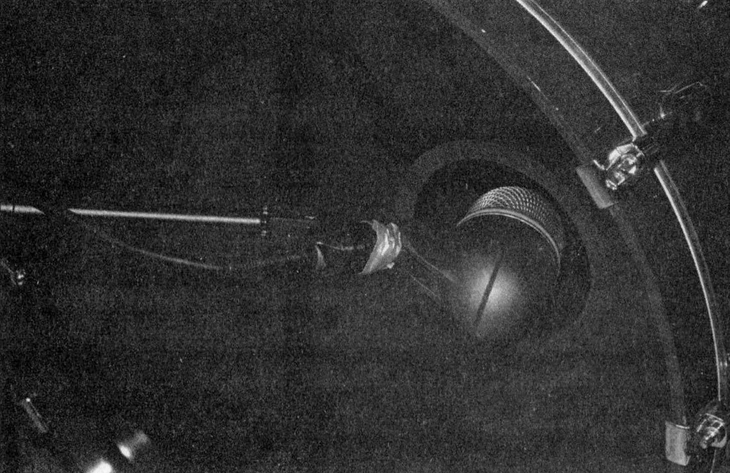

Figure 6.5: Placing The Mic In The Hole Of The Front Head

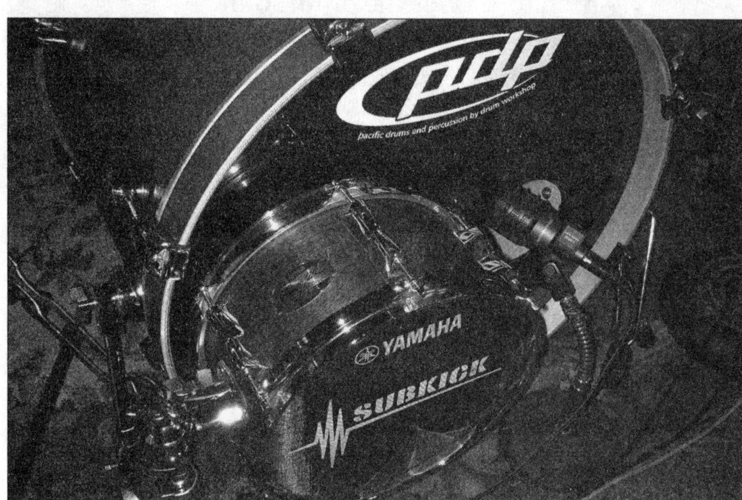

Figure 6.6: A Yamaha SKRM 100 Subkick Mic

The Subkick Mic

The subkick phenomena started recently due to the burning desire to get a little more of the lower-bass sound out of the kick without having to crank up the EQ. The subkick mic is actually a small speaker (anywhere from 5 to 8 inches) that's used as a microphone to pick up the ultra-lows (below 50Hz) of a kick drum that most mics just can't capture. While this is can be jury rigged by taking the low-frequency driver from a speaker like a Yamaha NS-10M, Yamaha also makes a commercial model known as the SKRM-100 (See Figure 6.6).

Making one of your own is easy. Just get a speaker and wire pins 2 and 3 of an XLR connector to the speaker's terminals (see Figure 6.7). The polarity might be backwards so be sure to check the Phase switch on the console or preamp to see which position has the most bottom.

E6.5: Placing The Subkick Mic

A) Place the subkick mic about 2 inches from the lip of the kick drum shell (see Figure 6.6). Listen on the monitors. Is there more low end? Is there more or less high end? Can you hear the sound of the beater?

B) Move the subkick back about three inches. Is there more or less low end? Can you hear any of the other drums leaking through?

Miking The Snare Drum

There must be a dozen ways to mic the snare drum, and if the snare sounds good in the first place, every one of them will work as far as sound goes. The thing about the snare is that you're trying to get the best isolation from the other drums as well, which can alter your approach a bit. The other thing is that you want to make sure that the mic is out of the way of the drummer so he doesn't hit it. Not only does that sound pretty bad, but it's not very good for mic either. Always ask if the drummer thinks if it will be in the way, and be prepared to move it to where he thinks it won't be hit.

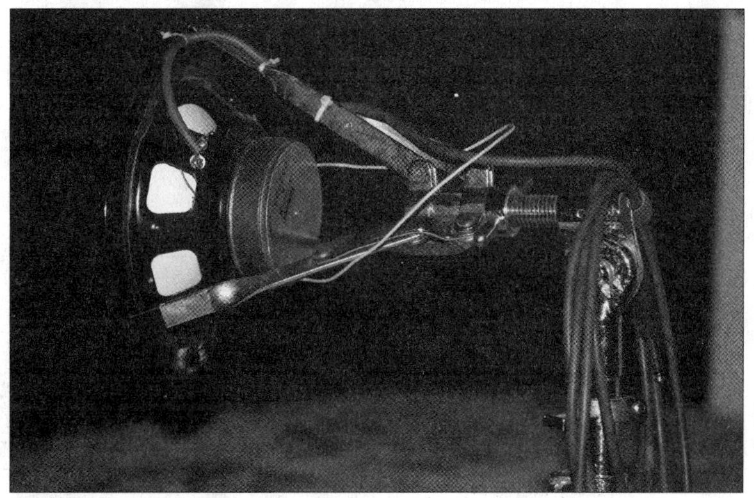

Figure 6.7: A Home-made Subkick Mic

Since the mic is placed so close to an extremely loud instrument like the snare (especially with a heavy hitter), it has to be able to handle a lot of level without distorting. That's one of the reason why the Shure SM57 has been such a go-to snare mic for so many engineers. There are plenty of other engineers who love small diaphragm condenser mics though, so don't be afraid to try one if you have it, but be sure to use the 10 or 20 dB pad so they won't overload.

E6.6: Miking The Snare Drum

A) Place the mic stand somewhere between the rack tom and hi-hats so it's out of the way of the drummer, and position it so it's about one inch, or about two of your fingers, above the rim. Point the mic towards the center of the drum head (see Figure 6.8). Make sure that the mic stand isn't touching any drum hardware to prevent the mic from picking up any unwanted vibrations.

B) Listen on the monitors. Does the drum sound tight and punchy? Does it have enough low end? Are there a lot of overtones? Is there a decay after the drum is hit or does it stop abruptly?

C) Point the mic closer to the rim of the snare. Listen on the monitors. Does the snare sound different? Is there more or less low end? Is there more or less high end? Are there more or fewer overtones? Can you hear the snares better or worse?

D) Point the mic across the top of the drum towards the far end of the rim. Listen on the monitors. Does the snare sound different? Is there more or less low end? Is there more or less high end? Are there more or fewer overtones? Can you hear the snares better or worse?

E) Place the mic where it has the best combination of body and snare sound.

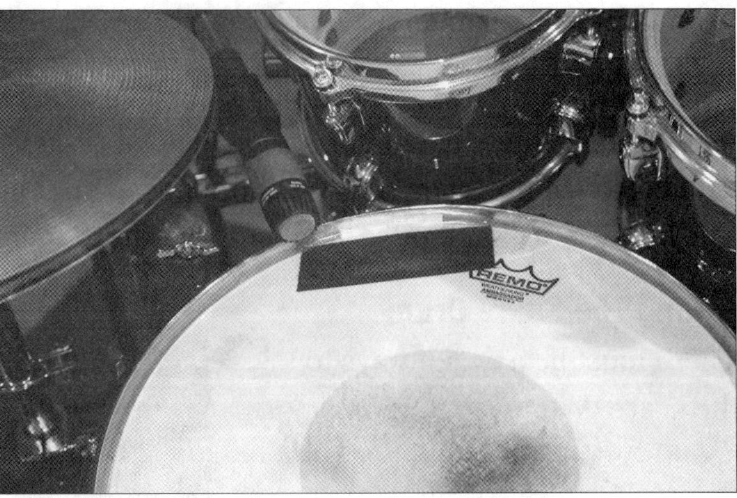
Figure 6.8: Mic Position For The Snare Drum

Snare Drum Bottom Head Miking

Sometimes the top snare mic just doesn't capture enough of the snap of the snare strainers, so a second mic is added under the drum pointing up at the them. Most of the time this mic will require the phase to be inverted, so be sure to check the selection on the preamp or console.

Figure 6.9: Placing A Mic Underneath The Snare

Although any mic will work as an under-snare mic, the more directional it is, the better—that way it won't pick up leakage from the bass drum. One favorite for the application is the Sennheiser MD-441, which is somewhat expensive and not found in many studios, but any cardioid mic (preferably hypercardioid) will work.

E6.7: Placing A Mic Underneath the Snare

A) Place the under-snare mic about six inches from the snare strainers as in Figure 6.9 and raise the level of the channel. Does the snare drum have more snap? Does it sound thin?

B) Insert a pad on the mic if available. Does it sound cleaner?

C) Select the low-frequency roll-off if available. Can you hear more or less of the kick drum?

D) Select each position of the Phase button either on your console or DAW. Which position has the fullest sound? That's the position to keep.

Miking The High-Hat

You might think that because there's so much high-hat leakage into the snare mic that a separate hat mic isn't necessary, but it's really nice to have when you need just a little more hat sparkle, or you just need a bit more hat level during a section of the song. Once again, there are a number of ways to mic the hat, but this way will not only sound good but provide some good isolation from the rest of the drums as well.

Most drummers use relatively heavy high-hats (especially if they use them for live gigging) which are on the dull sounding side, so a mic that favors the high-end and responds well to the transient nature of the cymbals works very well. That's why a small diaphragm condenser mic is usually used, although the mic doesn't matter as much as the placement.

Figure 6.10: Hi-Hat Mic Placement

Figure 6.11: Mic Placement For A Thinner Hat Sound

Figure 6.12: DON'T Mic The High-Hat This Way

E6.8: High-Hat Mic Positioning

A) Make sure that the mic is placed towards the rear of the kit as far away from the crash cymbal as possible.

B) Place the mic about halfway between the bell and the edge of the top cymbal, pointing directly down.

C) Position the mic up about six inches over the top cymbal in the open position, as this position picks up more of the overall tone of the cymbals (see Figure 6.10). Have the drummer play the hat and listen in the control room. Note the sound.

D) Move the mic closer to the hat so it's about three inches from the top cymbal in the open position. Does it sound thicker or thinner? Do you hear more or fewer overtones? Return the mic to its original position.

E) Move the mic out towards the edge of the top hat as in Figure 6.11. Does it sound thicker or thinner? Do you hear more or fewer overtones?

F) Place the mic right on the edge looking in at the hat as in Figure 6.12. Do you hear a puff of air? Does it sound thicker or thinner? Do you hear more or fewer overtones?

G) Return the mic to its position in A if you haven't found a better sounding place.

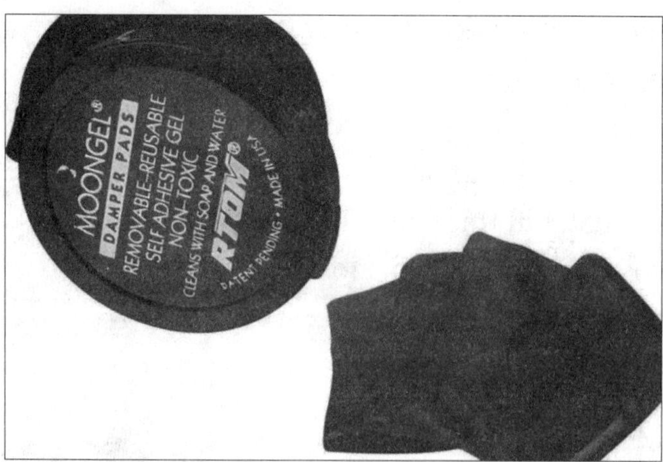
Figure 6.13: Moongel Damper Pads

Miking The Toms

Once again, the key to a big powerful tom sound is the sound of the toms themselves. Do what you need to do to make them sound great acoustically first! You can use a little black electrical tape or Moongel (see Figure 6.13) to take out the ringing if you think that sounds better, but remember, the ring is part of the sound too. As with all padding, use it sparingly and don't deaden them up too much, unless that's the effect you're looking for.

Figure 6.14: Rack Tom Mic Position

While many engineers use a dynamic mic like a Sennheiser MD 421, a condenser mic like an AKG 414, AKG 451, or a Shure KSM44 provides a nice full sound. Be sure to switch on the -10 dB pad and select the cardioid position. Check with the drummer before you mount anything on his kit and to make sure that the mics are out of his way.

E6.9: Rack Tom Mic Positioning

A) Place the mic about six inches above the drum head, just over the rim, pointing toward the center of the head to get the most attack as in Figure 6.14. Have the drummer play the tom and listen in the control room. Note the sound. Can you hear any ring? Does it sound big or thin? Can you hear the attack of the stick hitting the drum? Can you hear the cymbals?

B) Point the mic towards the edge of the head. Do you hear more or less ring? Does it sound bigger or thinner? Can you hear the attack of the stick hitting the drum? Do you hear more or less cymbal leakage? Return the mic to its starting position.

C) Move the mic so it's about three inches from the head. Do you hear more or less ring? Does it sound bigger or thinner? Can you hear the attack of the stick hitting the drum? Do you hear more or less cymbal leakage? Return the mic to its original position.

D) Move the mic so it's about nine inches from the head. Do you hear more or less ring? Does it sound bigger or thinner? Can you hear the attack of the stick hitting the drum? Do you hear more or less cymbal leakage?

E) Return the mic to its position in A if you haven't found a better sounding place.

E6.10: Floor-Tom Mic Positioning

A) Place the mic about six inches above the drum head, just over the rim, pointing toward the center of the head as in Figure 6.15. Make sure that the mic is as far away from the cymbal and snare drum as you can place it. Have the drummer play the tom and listen in the control room. Note the sound. Can you hear any ring? Does it sound big or thin? Can you hear the attack of the stick hitting the drum? Can you hear the cymbals?

B) Point the mic towards the edge of the head near the rim. Do you hear more or less ring? Does it sound bigger or thinner? Can you hear the attack of the stick hitting the drum? Do you hear more or less cymbal leakage? Return the mic to its starting position.

C) Move the mic so it's about three inches from the head. Do you hear more or less ring? Does it sound bigger or thinner? Can you hear the attack of the stick hitting the drum? Do you hear more or less cymbal leakage? Return the mic to its original position.

D) Move the mic so it's about nine inches from the head. Do you hear more or less ring? Does it sound bigger or thinner? Can you hear the attack of the stick hitting the drum? Do you hear more or less cymbal leakage?

E) Return the mic to its position in A if you haven't found a better sounding place.

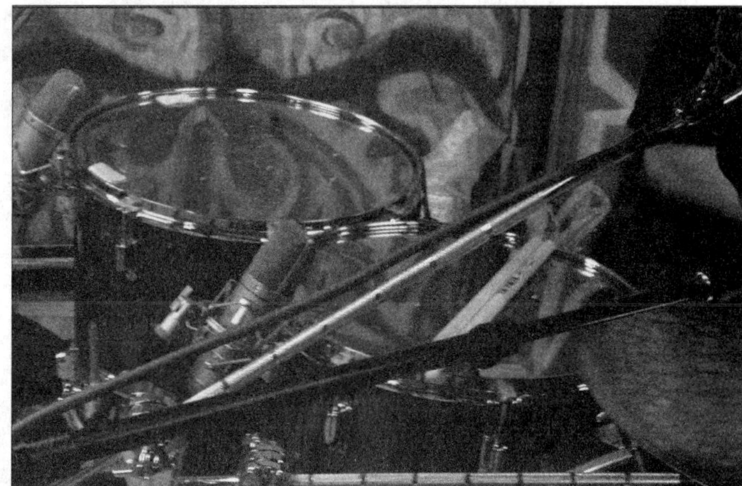

Figure 6.15: Floor Tom Mic

Miking The Cymbals

The overheads are used to pick up the ride and crash cymbals and give you an ambient stereo sound of the drum kit. There are a few ways to mic overheads, depending on how "live" your room is. If you have a very live room, you may want your overheads closer to the kit to reduce the amount of room ambiance that's being picked up.

Cymbals are loud so make sure you switch on the -10 dB pad if you're using condenser mics, and select any high-pass filter since it will help the sound of the cymbals to be heard more clearly. Don't worry that you're not getting a totally isolated cymbal sound in these channels because the overhead mics are meant to add an overall ambient sound of the drum kit to the mix.

E6.11: Miking The Cymbals With Overhead Position One

A) Place the left and right mics parallel to each other over the bell of the crash cymbal on each side of the drum kit at a height of about 18 inches, pointing down over the bell of the crash cymbal (see Figure 6.16). Have the drummer play just the cymbals while you listen on the monitors. Can you hear each cymbal? Is one louder than the rest? If so, move the position of the mic away from the loud cymbal to try to equalize the volume.

B) Move the mics away from the bell. Is the sound thicker or thinner? Can you hear the cymbals "swishing" as they rock back and forth, getting nearer and further from the mic?

C) Move the mics to about half as close as they were in A. Is the sound thicker or thinner? Can you hear more or less swishing? Is the cymbal balance better or worse? Return them to the original position.

D) Move the mics to about 24 inches away from the cymbals. Is the sound thicker or thinner? Can you hear more or less swishing? Is the cymbal balance better or worse? Return them to the original position.

E) Have the drummer play the song that you're about to record. Can you hear the drum kit leakage into the cymbal mics? Is the leakage clear and distinct or dull and fuzzy sounding?

F) Return the mics to their position in A if you haven't found a better sounding place.

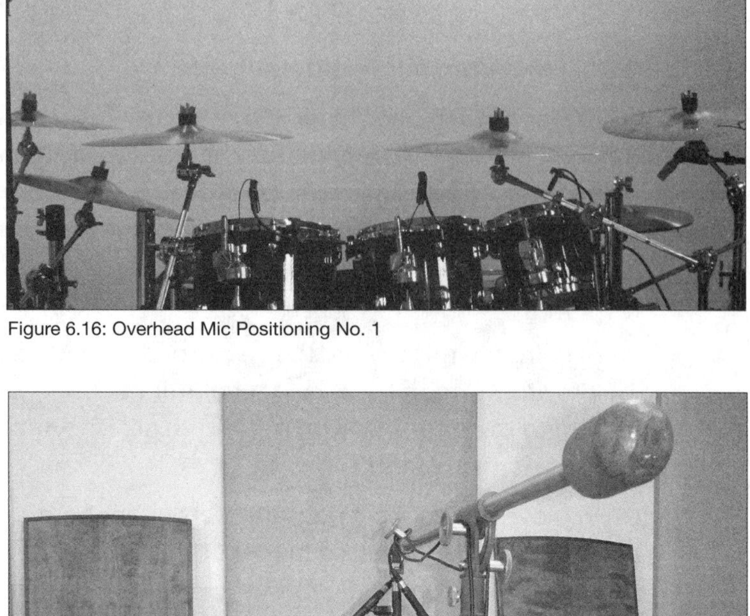

Figure 6.16: Overhead Mic Positioning No. 1

Figure 6.17: Mojave Audio M100s Used For ORTF Overhead Miking

Overhead Position Two

While Overhead Position One is used mainly for miking mostly the cymbals, Overhead Position Two is designed to pick up the entire drum kit. In this configuration, two mikes are crossed at about a 110° angle (see Figure 6.17) and about 7 inches apart, which is called ORTF (we'll talk about this technique more in Chapter 10).

The setup for Position Two is a little more difficult in that you'll need two heavy duty boom stands and some patience to position the mics correctly, or a stereo positioning bar that's specially made for this purpose (see Figure 6.18).

E6.12: Miking The Cymbals With Overhead Position Two

A) Place two identical directional microphones in the ORTF configuration (see Figure 6.17) over the exact center of the drum kit about a foot over the drummer's head.

B) Adjust the gain so it's the same for both mics and pan them hard left and right. Have the drummer play the song you're about to record and listen in the control room. Do you hear just the cymbals or the entire kit? Is the sound of the kit balanced or are some drums missing or louder than others?

C) Lower the ORTF configuration so it's about even with the top of the drummer's head. Do you hear just the cymbals or the entire kit? Is the sound of the kit balanced or are some drums missing or louder than others? Return the mics to their original position.

D) Raise the ORTF configuration so it's about two feet over the drummer's head. Do you hear just the cymbals or the entire kit? Is the sound of the kit balanced or are some drums missing or louder than others? Do you hear more or less of the room ambiance.

E) Return the mics to their original position.

Overhead Position One usually works best when you're recording in a small room with a low ceiling (10 feet high or less) since the mics are closer to the cymbals and there's less reflection from the ceiling. Overhead Position Two doesn't usually work well with low ceilings.

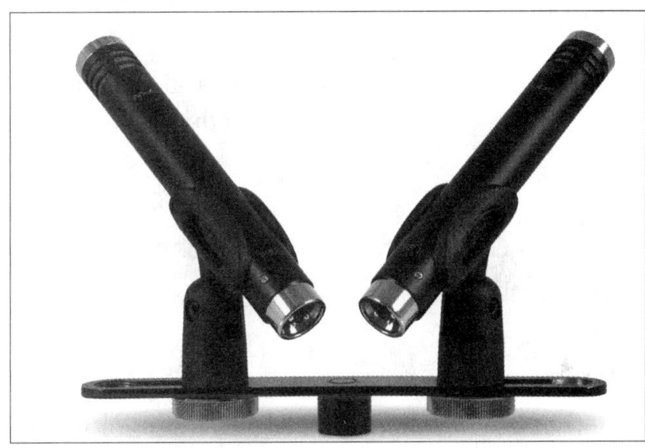

Figure 6.18: M-Audio Pulsar Mics On A Stereo Bar

Miking The Room

Room mics are used to glue the drums all together by filling in the frequency holes to make the individual drums sound more like a a single complete drumset. What you're going for is a sound that's exactly the same as when you're standing in front of the kit.

Some engineer's use a single room mic while others may use three: left, right, and center. Since you normally don't use that much of the room mic in the mix unless the room sounds particularly good, we'll just use one mic aimed at the center of the drum kit for our example. If you decide to use stereo room mics, place a mic at each side of the kit about ten feet apart and looking directly at the outside edge of the furthest cymbal.

E6: 13: Placing The Room Mic

A) Place a directional mic about six feet away from the drum kit at a height about equal to the drummer's eyes. Point the mic down at the snare drum or the top edge of the bass drum. Have the drummer play the song you're about to record and listen in the control room. Is the sound of the kit balanced or are some drums missing or louder than others?

B) Replace the mic with a different directional mic. Did the sound change? Is the sound of the kit balanced or are some drums missing or louder than others? Can you hear more of less of the room ambiance? Is there more or less low end? Is there more or less high end?

C) Replace the mic with an omnidirectional mic. Did the sound change? Is the sound of the kit balanced or are some drums missing or louder than others? Can you hear more of less of the room ambiance? Is there more or less low end? Is there more or less high end? Choose the mic that you think sounds best.

D) Point the mic lower so that it's aiming at the middle of the bass drum. Did the sound change? Is the sound of the kit balanced or are some drums missing or louder than others? Can you hear more of less of the room ambiance? Is there more or less low end? Is there more or less high end?

E) Move the mic back back to about ten feet away from the drum kit. Did the sound change? Is the sound of the kit balanced or are some drums missing or louder than others? Can you hear more of less of the room ambiance? Is there more or less low end? Is there more or less high end? Return the mic to its original position.

F) Move the mic in so it's about three feet away from the drum kit. Did the sound change? Is the sound of the kit balanced or are some drums missing or louder than others? Can you hear more of less of the room ambiance? Is there more or less low end? Is there more or less high end?

G) Move the mic backwards or forwards until you find the position where the kit is the most balanced.

Sound Check

Now that you've placed all of the microphones and experimented with different positions and approaches, it's time to have a listen and to see what you have. For each drum that you're checking, have the drummer do a steady slow beat on that drum only at about one hit per second. You don't want it hit too quickly because you want to hear the decay of the sound.

Individual Drum Sound Check

The best way to approach getting a certain drum sound is to think of the drum kit as a single instrument instead of 7 or 8 separate drums. Listen for a unified overall sound with no one element standing out from the rest. The drum mix is all about the balance between the drums and then the balance against the rest of the band.

Exercise Pod: Drum Sound Check

E6: 14: Getting The Kick Drum Sound

A) Have the drummer begin with even hits on the kick drum about a second apart so you can hear the decay.

B) Raise the level of the monitors to moderately loud.

C) Raise the level of the kick drum channel so you can hear it in the monitors. How does it sound? Is it thin sounding? Is it bottom heavy? Is it distorted? Are there any crackles? Are there any mechanical noises from the drums?

D) Regardless whether the kick drum has a front head or not, aim the mic more at the beater for more definition. Aim it a few inches away if the beater is too loud. Is there more or less definition from the kick? Can you hear more or less of the beater?

E) If the drum needs more body, move the mic away from the head in 3 inch increments.

F) Try a different mic in the same position. Is the sound bigger and fuller? Does it have more definition?

G) Mute or lower the kick drum channel.

E6: 15: Getting The Snare Drum Sound

A) Have the drummer begin with even hits on the snare drum about a second apart so you can hear the decay.

B) Raise the level of the monitors to moderately loud.

C) Raise the level of the snare drum channel. How does it sound? Is it thin sounding? Is it bottom heavy? Is it distorted? Are there any crackles? Can you hear any mechanical noises? Do the toms ring when the snare is hit?

D) Aim the mic closer to the rim instead of at the middle. Does it sound fuller? Is there as much definition?

E) Aim the mic at the rim on the other side of the drum. Does it sound fuller? Is there as much definition? Is it thinner sounding?

F) Try a different mic in all three positions. Is the sound bigger and fuller? Does it have more definition?

G) Try putting a piece of tape on the drum. Is there more or less ring?

H) Mute or lower the snare drum channel.

E6: 16: Getting The Rack Tom Sound

A) Have the drummer begin with even hits on the rack tom about a second apart so you can hear the decay.

B) Raise the level of the monitors to moderately loud.

C) Raise the level of the rack tom channel. How does it sound? Is it thin sounding? Is it bottom heavy? Is it distorted? Are there any crackles? Can you hear any mechanical noises?

D) Aim the mic closer to the rim instead of at the middle. Does it sound fuller? Is there as much definition?

E) Raise the mic about 3 inches higher. Does it sound fuller? Can you hear more overtones? Is there as much definition? Is it thinner sounding?

F) Try a different mic in the same positions. Is the sound bigger and fuller? Does it have more definition?

G) Mute or lower the tom channel and go on to the next rack tom, if there is one.

E6: 17: Getting The Floor Tom Sound

A) Have the drummer begin with even hits on the floor tom about a second apart so you can hear the decay.

B) Raise the level of the monitors to moderately loud.

C) Raise the level of the floor tom channel. How does it sound? Is it thin sounding? Is it bottom heavy? Is it distorted? Are there any crackles? Can you hear any mechanical noises?

D) Aim the mic closer to the rim instead of at the middle. Does it sound fuller? Is there as much definition?

E) Raise the mic about 3 inches higher. Does it sound fuller? Can you hear more overtones? Is there as much definition? Is it thinner sounding?

F) Try a different mic in the same positions. Is the sound bigger and fuller? Does it have more definition?

G) Mute or lower the floor tom channel.

E6: 18: Getting The Cymbal Sound

A) Have the drummer hit the cymbals on the left and then the right side of the kit about a second apart.

B) Raise the level of the monitors to a moderately loud level.

C) Raise the level of both cymbal channels. How does it sound? Is it thin sounding? Is it bottom heavy? Are the cymbals balanced? Is it distorted? Are there any crackles?

D) If the cymbals are out of balance on either side, move the mic closer to the quietest one.

E) If one of the cymbals seems to swoosh as it vibrates, move the mic closer to the bell.

F) Try a set of different mics in the same positions. Is the sound bigger and fuller? Does it have more definition?

G) Mute or lower the cymbal channels.

E6: 19: Getting The High-Hat Sound

A) Have the drummer play the high-hat part to the song.

B) Raise the level of the monitors to moderately loud.

C) Raise the level of the hat channel. How does it sound? Is it thin sounding? Is it bottom heavy? Are the cymbals balanced? Is it distorted? Are there any crackles?

D) If the hat sounds too thick, move it towards the lip of the cymbal. If it's too thin sounding, move it more towards the bell.

E) Raise the mic about 3 inches higher. Does it sound fuller? Can you hear more overtones? Is there as much definition? Is it thinner sounding?

F) Try a different mic in the same positions. Is the sound bigger and fuller? Does it have more definition?

G) Mute or lower the high-hat channel.

E6: 20: Getting The Room Mic Sound

A) Have the drummer play a beat.

B) Raise the level of the monitors to moderately loud.

C) Raise the level of the room mics. How does it sound? Is it thin sounding? Is it bottom heavy? Is there too much room? Is it distorted? Are there any crackles?

D) If the room boings or if it's too live, move the room mics closer to the kick in about 3 foot increments.

E) Try a different mic in the same positions. Is the sound bigger and fuller? Does it have more definition?

F) Mute or lower the room mic channels.

Checking The Drum Phase

This was already discussed in Chapter 5 but it's important enough to cover one more time. One of the most important yet overlooked parts of a drum mix is checking the phase of the drums. This is important because not only will an out-of-phase channel suck the low end out of the mix, but it will get more difficult to fix as the mix progresses.

A drum mic can be out of phase due to a mis-wired cable or poor mic placement. Either way, it's best to fix it now before the mix goes any further.

Exercise Pod: Checking The Drum Phase

E6.21: Checking The Drum Phase

A) With all the drums in the mix, go to the kick drum channel and change the selection of the polarity or phase control (see Figure 6.19). Is there more low end or less? Chose the selection with the most bottom end.

B) Go to the snare drum channel and change the selection of the polarity or phase control. Is there more low end or less? Chose the selection with the most bottom end.

C) Go to each tom mic channel and change the selection of the polarity or phase control. Is there more low end or less? Chose the selection with the most bottom end.

D) Go to each cymbal mic or overhead mic and change the selection of the polarity or phase control. Is there more low end or less? Chose the selection with the most bottom end.

E) Go to each room mic channel and change the selection of the polarity or phase control. Is there more low end or less? Chose the selection with the most bottom end.

Getting The Overall Drum Sound

Once you've gotten the sound of the individual drums, it's time to listen to the total drum kit and get a mix together. There are several schools of thought about which drum to start the drum mix from, but we'll start with what is probably the standard: the kick drum. Wherever you start from, the idea is to blend all the different drum mics into a cohesive single drum sound.

Figure 6.19: The Phase Control On A Console Or Mixer

E6: 22: Getting The Overall Drum Sound

A) Stand about 6 feet in front of the kit and listen while the drummer plays the song you're about to record. Note the balance of the kit.

B) Raise the level of the kick drum until it reads about -10 dB on the master mix bus meter.

C) Raise the level of the snare until it's about the same level. Did the sound of the kick change when it was paired with the snare? Is the kick masked by the snare and no longer distinct? How high does the master mix bus meter read?

D) Go to a place in the song where there are tom fills. Raise the level of all toms until they're about the same level as the kick and snare. Did the sound of the kick and/or snare change? Do the kick and snare sound different when the toms aren't playing? How high does the master mix bus meter read?

E) Raise the level of the cymbal or overhead mics until the overall sound begins to change and the cymbals become more distinct sounding. What happened to the sound of the other drums? How high does the master mix bus meter read? Do the cymbals overpower the rest of the drums?

F) You can probably hear the high hat already, but raise the level of the high-hat mic until it becomes a bit more distinct sounding. Does the sound of the snare change? Does the sound of any of the toms or cymbals change? How high does the master mix bus meter read?

G) Bring up the room mic(s) to the point where you can just hear them. This will fill in the sound a lot and glue together the kit balance. What happened to the sound of the other drums? How high does the master mix bus meter read? Is it bigger or smaller sounding

Panning The Drums

There are two ways to pan the drums: from an audience viewpoint as you stand in front of them, or from the drummer's viewpoint. Most engineers use the audience perspective and that's what we're used to hearing on records, which means that with a right-handed drummer the hi-hat would be panned to the right, the snare would be just off-center to the right (leaving it in the center is okay too), the floor tom to the left, and the bass drum would be centered.

E6.23: Panning The Drums

A) Pan the snare slightly off center to the right as you see it.

B) Pan the high-hat to about 3 o'clock, as you see it.

C) For a three tom kit, pan the high rack tom to the right at 3 o'clock, the next lower tom to the center at 12 o'clock, and the lowest tom to the left at 9 o'clock for a nice stereo spread.

D) Sometimes setting the panning a little narrower at 10 and 2 o'clock centers the drums a little better.

E) Overheads are usually panned hard right and the left, although the track sometimes benefits if those are pulled in to the 9 and 3 o'clock positions as well.

F) Pan the room mic to the center. For stereo room mics, pan them the same as the overheads.

Tweaking The Drum Sound

After you've gotten a balance and have moved the mics around to get the best sound possible, you still might find you need to tweak the sound a bit with a little EQ and compression. *Little* is the operative word here in that if you feel you require more than 3 dB of equalization or compression then something is radically wrong and you should either tune the drum, or try a different mic or placement.

Using The EQ During Drum Tracking

The reason why you'll use any EQ at all is for definition of the drum sound, not to "make it sound better." If it doesn't already sound great in the room when you listen, chances are you can't help the sound much, but you can make it so you hear each drum clearer. While you can use the subtractive EQ method from Chapter 4, here are some frequencies to tweak on the different drums that will help you do that.

Exercise Pod: Tweaking The Drum Sound

E6.24: EQing The Drums

A) Attenuate the kick by 3 dB at 400 to 500Hz. Does it sound less boxy? Adjust to taste.

B) Attenuate the kick by 3 dB at 1.5kHz. Does it song less "honky"? Adjust to taste.

C) Add 3 dB at 80Hz to the kick. Does it sound bigger or fuller? Adjust to taste.

D) Add 3 dB at 5kHz. Does it have more definition? Adjust to taste.

E) Add 3 dB at 10–12kHz to the snare. Is it crisper sounding? Can you hear the snare strainers more? Adjust to taste.

F) Add 3 dB at 125Hz to the snare. Is it fuller sounding? Adjust to taste.

G) Add 3 dB at 1kHz to the snare. Does it have more definition? Adjust to taste.

H) Add 3 dB at 10kHz to the high hat. Does it have more sizzle? Adjust to taste.

I) Filter out everything below 160kHz using the high-pass filter on the console or preamp on the hat. Does it have more definition? Do you lose the bottom end? Adjust to taste.

J) Attenuate 1kHz by 3 dB on the high hat. Does it have more definition? Is it thinner sounding? Does it fit into the mix better? Adjust to taste.

K) Add 3 dB at 200 to 400Hz to the rack toms. Do they sound fuller? Do they fit into the track better? Adjust to taste.

L) Add 3 dB at 5kHz to the rack toms. Do they have more definition? Adjust to taste.

M) Attenuate 3 dB at 150 to 500Hz from the floor tom. Does it still sound like a beach ball? Adjust to taste.

N) Add 3 dB at 10kHz to the cymbals. Do they have more sizzle? Adjust to taste.

O) Filter out everything below 160kHz using the high-pass filter on the console or preamp on the hat. Do they have more definition? Do you lose the bottom end? Adjust to taste.

Using The Compressor/Limiter During Drum Tracking

You have to be careful when compressing during tracking because, just like EQ, if you overdo it you can't change it later. If you find that your drummer has an uneven hitting technique on the kick and snare, a little compression (about 2 dB) helps to even it out. If you have any doubts about how and why to use compression, leave it for mixing later.

E6.25: Compressing The Drums

A) Start with a 4:1 ratio and with a fast release and a quick attack. Set the *Threshold* so there's about 2 dB of compression. Does the meter seem to be moving with the pulse of the song? If not, make the release time shorter. Does the drum sound like it's lost some high end? If so, make the attack time longer.

B) Increase the ratio to 12:1. Did the sound change? Did the amount of compression change? Adjust to taste.

C) Increase the Threshold until there's about 6 dB of compression. Did the sound change? Did the hits get more even? Adjust to taste.

D) If in doubt, don't use the compressor.

The Recording Drummer

Many drummers that don't have a lot of studio experience aren't sure of exactly what they should bring to a session and what they should do when they get there. Here's a little guidance that you can tell them in order to make your job easier.

- **Change your heads.** Nothing will help the sound of your drums like new heads. Get a set of new heads (at least the top ones) and either change them before you get to the studio or make sure that you have enough time to do so before recording.

- **Make sure your drums are in tune.** Tune your drums as described above or hire someone that really knows how to do it. Not only will you learn something but you'll get a much better sounding recording as a result.

- **Bring all your snare drums to the session.** You never know if and when a particular snare is right for a song until you try it. Sometimes you can be surprised about how good or how bad a drum sounds in the context of a recording, so to be safe, bring as many snares as you can to the session.

- **Bring extra heads, sticks, beaters, cymbals, and batteries.** Just like on-stage, this is the professional thing to do. You have to have backups in case you break a head, or the battery on your metronome dies. Even if you usually only play with a certain type of stick, bring several kinds (plus mallets and brushes) since that could be the perfect sound for the track you're recording. Even if you think you have everything in your case or gig box, double check to make sure. It's easy to forget the last time you broke a head and never replaced the replacement.

CHAPTER 7
RECORDING GUITAR AND BASS

If it were as easy as just placing a mic in one standard spot, then getting great guitar and bass sounds would never be much of a problem, but we all know that's not the case. Capturing the sound of an electric or acoustic guitar or bass can sometimes be madly frustrating, because unfortunately, recording the sound that you hear in the room is not always as easy as it seems. Of course, the player, the gear, the song, the arrangement and the studio all play a hand in getting a great sound, but here are some ways to get a better guitar sound almost every time.

Electric Guitar Recording

Electric guitar recording has evolved through the years, from miking the amplifier from a distance, to close miking, to using multiple mics, to recording direct and finally using an amplifier emulator. No one technique is better than another. In fact, multiple techniques are frequently used on the same recording.

Electric guitars don't need anything fancy to capture their sound. The frequency response doesn't go that high or that low, and the more distorted it is, the fewer transients the signal has, making it somewhat easier to capture than other instruments. As a result, dynamic mics are frequently used with good results. That said, sometimes it's surprising just how good an amp can sound when a large diaphragm condenser or ribbon mic is used, so don't be afraid to experiment.

Miking The Amplifier

While many engineers like to use our friend the Shure SM57 in this role, just about any mic can work if you know the sound that you're looking for and the best way to approach it.

Exercise Pod: Recording The Electric Guitar

E7.1: Miking The Amplifier

A) If there are two or more speakers in the cabinet, listen to them all to find the one that sounds the best. Is one scratchy sounding or distorted? Is one muffled with no high end? Does one have no low end? Find the one with the best balance of frequencies that's not intentionally distorted.

Figure 7.1: The Classic Setup: An SM57 On Guitar Cabinet

B) Place the mic about one inch away from the best sounding speaker in the cabinet and about three quarters of the way between the edge of the speaker and the voice coil (the center of the speaker—see Figure 7.1). Have the guitar player play the song you're about to record, and listen on the monitors. Does it sound like what you heard in the room? Is the sound full enough? Is it too edgy? Is it too bassy?

C) Move the mic towards the voice coil. Is the sound still full? Did it get brighter? Did it get bassy?

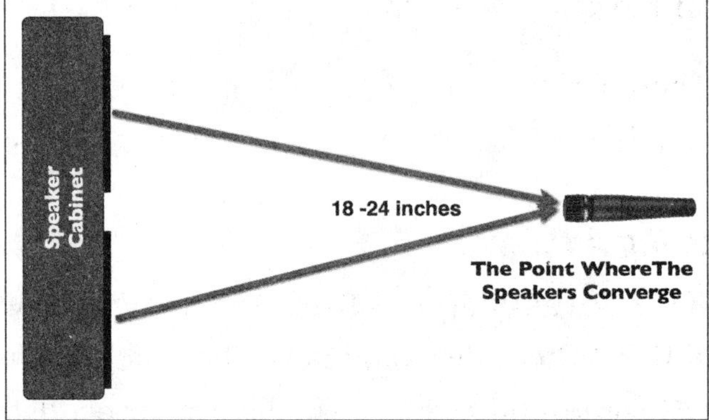

Figure 7.2: Classic Setup Two: Distance Miking Where The Speakers Converge

D) Move the mic towards the outside edge of the speaker. Is the sound still full? Did it brighter? Did it get bassy?

E) Move the mic about at least a foot away from the the speaker or speakers to capture some of the room sound. The ideal distance on a cabinet with two speakers is where the output of both speakers combine (see Figure 7.2). Does it sound bigger? Can you hear the sound of the room in the recording? Can you hear some frequencies cancel out between the two speakers?

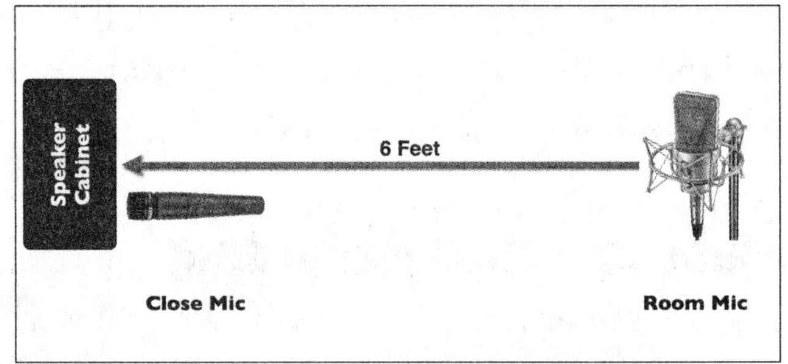

Figure 7.3: Additional Distance Mic Added To Close Mic

F) Move the mic to the side to capture more of one of the speaker's voice coils if more high end is required.

G) Move the mic back to the best sounding position close to the speaker and add an additional mic at the spot where the sound of the speakers converge 18 to 24 inches away (see Figure 7.3). Is the sound still full? Did it get brighter? Did it get bassy? Did it get bigger sounding? Is it closer to what you heard in the room? Is there more of the room sound?

H) Increase the distance to 6 feet if possible. Is the sound still full? Did it brighter? Did it get bassy? Is there more of the room sound?

I) Place both mics at the point where they give the sound closest to what you heard in the room, or what best fits the track when the other instruments are playing.

Recording The Guitar Direct

Once upon a time, plugging a guitar directly into the console was the last thing a guitar player wanted to do. Players hated the sound because the high-end was rolled off, and the output was just so wimpy that virtually no one thought it was usable.

That thinking began to change in the '80s when better direct boxes, mic preamps, and new direct recording techniques were developed. With the advent of multi-effects devices in the '90s (especially Line 6's *Pod*), direct recording has now become totally acceptable and in some cases even preferred to using an amp. Certainly from the convenience and sound variety aspects, there's no comparison to live recording as recording direct is now used by far more guitarists than not.

There are three methods of recording direct: plugging a guitar into a DI box, plugging an amp into a DI box, and plugging a guitar into an effects box. Let's look at them all.

Using A Direct Box

The real secret to getting a great sounding direct recording is compression, and plenty of it. When you use a tube-style guitar amplifier, there's already some compression built into the sound between the circuitry, the tubes, and the speakers. Unfortunately you don't have the benefit of any of this help when recording direct. That's why it's important to always use some compression to keep the sound at relatively the same level. Doing so makes it sound strong and stand on its own. Without compression, the sound will be weak and wimpy.

Many stand-alone microphone preamps now have guitar inputs that eliminate the need for a direct box. That said, the following still holds true.

E7.2: Recording The Guitar Through A Direct Box

A) After you've plugged the guitar into the direct box and the output of the box into a console, mic preamp, or DAW, flip the ground switch to find the quietest setting.

B) Play the guitar. What does it sound like? Does it sound full? Are the high frequencies rolled off? Is the sound aggressive or wimpy?

C) Plug a compressor either into the output of the mic preamp, or an insert on the console. Start with the compressor set to either a 4:1 or 8:1 compression ratio, with both the attack and release controls set to medium.

D) Set the *Threshold* control so there's at least 5 or 6 dB of compression happening. Does it sound fuller? Does it still sound wimpy?

E) What does it sound like with 20 dB of compression? Does it sound fuller? Does it still sound wimpy?

F) Depending upon the type of rhythm that you're playing, you may want to decrease both the attack and release time so they react faster, but be aware that the sound will begin to dull if the attack is too fast, and you'll begin to hear the compressor work if the release time is too short.

Direct From The Amp

While many of the newer amplifiers have outputs intended for direct recording, don't expect to get the same sound that you get from the speakers. You're hearing the sound of only the preamp section of the amplifier, which sounds nothing like an amp cranked through the speakers. If you treat this sound as just a slightly more effected clean direct signal however, you might find the sound very pleasing to work with. Keep in mind that the settings that you normally use on the amp might have to be changed in order to get a usable direct sound.

Another way to record direct, especially with an amp that doesn't have a direct output feature, is to feed a signal from the extension speaker jack of the amp into a direct box that's has the ability to accept this type of input (see Figure 7.4). Usually the DI will have two inputs: one labeled "Guitar" and the other labeled "Amp" or "Speaker." Make sure that, when using this method, you only connect to the Amp or Speaker input as the voltage coming from the extension speaker output is high enough to destroy the direct box if plugged into the Guitar input, and may even damage the amp as well in rare cases. As with the direct output from the amp, the sound will not be what you experience out of the speakers so you may have to adjust the amp's controls in order to get a sound that you find useful.

Figure 7.4: A Direct Box Speaker Switch

Through An Effects Box

Direct recording is no longer that big a deal since there are so many effects boxes and amplifier emulators on the market that are capable of acting as a sort of "super direct box" for recording. Starting with Line 6's *Pod* in 1998, just about every manufacturer now offers an inexpensive guitar box capable of direct recording. IK Multimedia has even launched the *iRig*, which allows recording directly to your iPhone or iPad (see Figure 7.5).

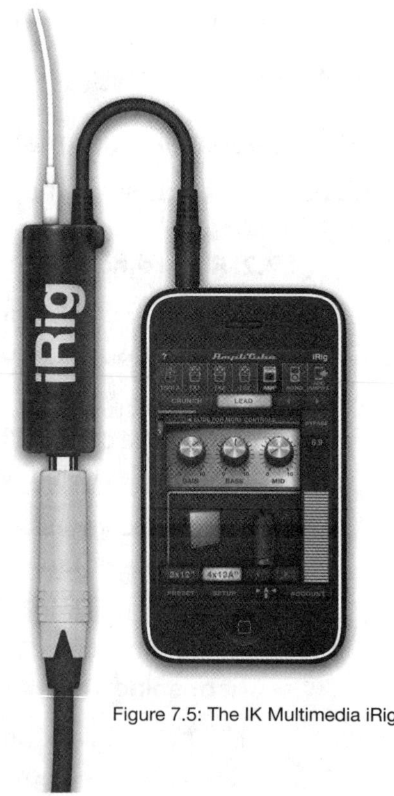

Figure 7.5: The IK Multimedia iRig

Regardless of which unit you use, keep the following in mind:

- **Be judicious with the distortion and sustain.** Lots of distortion and sustain is fun to play with, but isn't always appropriate for the song. Be prepared to dial it back to make your part fit better in the mix, especially if you'll be adding other guitar parts later.

- **Be judicious with the effects.** One of the cool things about modeling and multi-effects boxes is that you can get such a wide variety of sounds, some with over-the-top effects. Just like with distortion, think of what's appropriate for the song, not what feels fun to play with. Once again, take into account how everything will fit together in the mix, especially if you add additional parts.

Acoustic Guitar Recording

Acoustic instruments need space to resonate, breathe, and project, so they rarely respond well to extreme close-miking. While it might seem that the best place to mike the guitar is at the sound-hole, you'll find that the sound is generally too bassy from only that area. A nice combination of high and low frequencies usually comes from somewhere around where the neck and the body join together, but this varies from instrument to instrument.

Likewise, the type of microphone used to record an acoustic is critical to the sound. While a dynamic mic like an SM57 will certainly work and may sound wonderful in some cases, a condenser or ribbon microphone is better able to capture the transients of the acoustic that make it sound like it's in the room with you.

Also, like all acoustic instruments, the sound of the environment makes a huge difference in the sound of the recording. If the room doesn't sound that great, it will dictate the type of mic you choose because you'll want to pick up less ambiance in the recording. However, if the room does sound good but has too many reflections or echoes, your sound can end up sounding cloudy and less defined. You can sometimes overcome this by setting up on a rug instead of the hard floor to keep the reflections to a minimum.

Recording Preparation

Acoustic guitar recording requires a preparation that's different from just about any other instrument. Before you begin recording even the first note, there are a few steps you should take first.

- **Change Your Strings.** Putting on a fresh set of strings will not only help with the tuning but make the instrument resonate better. This results in a better recording.

- **Listen To The Room.** Listen to how the guitar resonates in the room you're playing in. Do a quick check of the room by loudly clapping your hands and listening for any unwanted echoes or flutters, then move to the smoothest sounding area.

- **Stand Back From The Instrument.** Move around the instrument to find the sweet spot where the direct sound of the guitar combines with the reflections of the room. Is the best sound on the neck, on the body, or both? Does your instrument resonate better a few feet back or up close?

• **Take Off Noisy Pieces Of Clothing.** Take off any watches, rings, jewelry, or belt buckles that may bang against the instrument. Also, certain jackets and/or shirts may have buttons that can cause a problem.

Exercise Pod: Recording The Acoustic Guitar

E7.3: Miking The Acoustic Guitar

A) Place the mic about 6 inches straight away from where the neck meets the body (see Figure 7.6). Listen on the monitors. Is the sound balanced? Is there too much bass? Is there enough definition? Does it sound like it does in the room?

B) Move the mic back to about 12 inches away. Is the sound balanced? Is there too much bass? Is there enough definition? Is there too much room?

C) Move the mic further towards the neck, pointed slightly down towards the higher strings. Is the sound balanced? Is there too much bass? Is there enough definition?

Figure 7.6: An Acoustic Guitar Miked By A Single Mic

D) Move it down towards the soundhole. Is the sound balanced? Is there too much bass? Is there enough definition?

E) Now move the mic directly over the soundhole. Is the sound balanced? Is there too much bass? Is there enough definition?

F) Move the mic back to about 24 inches away. Is the sound balanced? Is there too much bass? Is there enough definition? Is there too much room?

G) Move the mic back to A and add another mic on the body (see Figure 7.7). Is the sound

Figure 7.7: Neck And Body Miking

balanced better? Is there more low end? Is there enough definition? Is there too much room?

H) Move the soundhole mic further towards the neck to increase the brightness captured by that mic. Move it further towards the bridge to darken the tone.

I) Place the mics where they give you the best balance of body and definition, and balance between the direct and ambient room sound.

Electric Bass Recording

Back in the '60s and '70s, the way engineers recorded the electric bass was by miking the bass amp. As direct boxes became more and more available, the trend eventually swung the other way, with most bass recording done direct. Today it's very common to record a bass using a combination of both an amp and direct, which provides the best of both worlds. While the bass will sound full and warm with a direct box, the amp can add just enough edge to help the bass punch through a mix.

When using a direct box, be aware that they're not all created equal in that some will not give you the low fundamental of the bass that you expect when recording this way. Active DIs do a better job at this than passive, although some passive boxes (like the ones made by Radial) do an excellent job because of the large Jensen transformer used in the circuit.

Depending on the sound that fits the track best, mix the amp track with a DI track. The sound will change substantially depending upon the balance of the DI and miked amplifier. ALWAYS check the phase relationship between the amp and DI to make sure there's no cancellation of the low end. Flip the polarity switch to the position that has the most bottom. Also remember that there's no rule that says that you have to use both tracks, so don't hesitate to use just a single track if it sounds best in the mix.

E7.4: Miking The Bass Amp

A) Listen closely to the amp as the bass player plays. If there are multiple speakers, find the one that sounds the best, as in E7.1A.

B) Place a large diaphragm dynamic mic like D-112, RE-20, or B52 a little off-center and a couple of inches away from a cone of the best sounding speaker in the bass cabinet.

C) Move the mic across the cone. Is there a spot where it sounds particularly good? Keep the mic at that spot. Is the sound balanced frequency response-wise? Can you hear any of the room reflections?

D) Move the mic towards the end of the cone? Is there more low end? Is it more distinct sounding?

E) Move the mic towards the center of the speaker? Is there more low end? Is it more distinct sounding?

F) Move the mic about a feet away from the speaker. Is there more low end? Is it more distinct sounding?

G) Move the mic about 2 feet away from the speaker. Is there more low end? Is it more distinct sounding? Can you hear more of the room? Does it work with the rest of the instruments?

H) Raise the cabinet about a foot off the floor. Is there more low end? Is it more distinct sounding?

I) Place the mic where it gives you the best balance of body and definition, and balance between the direct and ambient room sound.

E7.5: Recording The Bass Direct

A) After you're plugged the bass into the direct box and the output of the box into a console, mic preamp, or DAW, flip the ground switch to find the quietest setting.

B) If used with an amp mic, raise the level of both amp and direct channels so they're equal in level. Flip the polarity switch to the position that has the most bottom.

C) Add a compressor/limiter if needed as in E7.2.

Recording The Acoustic Bass

The acoustic string bass is one of the hardest instruments to record for a variety of reasons. First, the tone depends largely upon the player. Second, mic placement is extremely important, and lastly, usually the bass is played in a live setting (like a jazz trio) where it's very close to other instruments, so there may be leakage from those instruments to contend with.

Mic position is everything when recording string bass. Just like with an acoustic guitar, close miking the F-hole makes the sound muddy with no definition, so another approach is needed. And perhaps more than any other instrument, the bass needs space to really sound right.

The type of mic used also has a big effect on the sound. Ribbon and condenser mics tend to sound better than dynamic mics in this application.

Figure 7.8: Royer R-121 On Upright Bass

E7.6: Recording The Acoustic Bass

A) Place a mic aimed below the bridge about 18 inches away (see Figure 7.8). Is the sound balanced frequency-wise? Is the sound boomy? Is there enough definition? Do you hear a lot of the room ambiance?

B) Move the mic so it's about 12 inches above the strings but pointed below the bridge

Figure 7.9: Soundelux U95 On Upright Bass

(see Figure 7.9). Is the sound balanced frequency-wise? Is the sound boomy? Is there enough definition? Do you hear a lot of the room ambiance?

C) Move the mic so it's about 18 inches away and even with the end of the fingerboard. Make sure it's pointed at about halfway between the fingerboard and the bridge. Is the sound balanced frequency-wise? Is the sound boomy? Is there enough definition? Do you hear a lot of the room ambiance?

D) Now move the mic to a place right above the right hand and point it towards the higher strings. Is the sound balanced frequency-wise? Is the sound boomy? Is there enough definition? Do you hear a lot of the room ambiance?

E) Choose the place that gives you the best tone and definition.

CHAPTER 8
VOCAL MIKING TECHNIQUES

Vocal recording in the studio can be a lot different from recording live. You're looking more for tonal quality and not sound pressure level, for one thing, so the miking technique is different. And you're looking for a great performance, which requires an environment that's carefully adjusted to make the vocalist comfortable. It's a common misperception that all you have to do is set up an expensive vintage microphone and everything will happen by itself, but it's not as easy as that (we all wish it were). It takes some technique, and some psychology, to help magic happen.

Recording Lead Vocals

The lead vocal is the focal point of most songs so it's normally approached with a bit more care than other instruments, both from a technical and a comfort standpoint. While the sound is important, it's the performance that really makes it work, so the singer's comfort level is always foremost in the engineer's mind. Let's look at some of the things involved in recording a killer vocal.

The Scratch Vocal

While experienced studio players can cut a great track without a guide or "scratch" vocal, almost every player would prefer to have one to play against when tracking. The guide vocal not only acts as a cue for certain sections of the song, but adds to the groove and feel that helps a player perform at his best. One of the other advantages is that the lead singer can also give directions and reminders to the players as the song progresses.

There are no particular rules for a scratch vocal. Some vocalists don't mind being in a vocal booth while performing a scratch vocal, but almost all vocalists want to be able to see all the players during a song as they dislike feeling disconnected from the rest of the band. As a result, many singers would actually prefer to be out in the room with the other players. The scratch track won't sound as good in that situation due to the leakage (mostly from the drums), but if it helps the performance of the band and vocalist, that's what you want to do.

Don't take a scratch vocal lightly and believe that it will be redone at a latter time under better conditions, because sometimes a little bit of magic happens that can't be recaptured again. Treat this vocal seriously because you never know when you might capture lightning in a bottle.

Finding The Right Placement In The Room

Where the singer is placed in the room makes a big difference in the sound. In general, vocals sound better when recorded in a tighter space, but many vocal booths not only feel tight but sound very closed as well. Low ceiling rooms can also be a problem with loud singers as they cause the room to ring at certain lower mid range frequencies.

That's why it's important to move the vocal into the biggest part of the studio for a vocal overdub, if possible. All vocals and instruments sound best when there's some space for the sound to develop. You can cut down on any unwanted reflections from the room by place baffles around singer (see Figure 8.1).

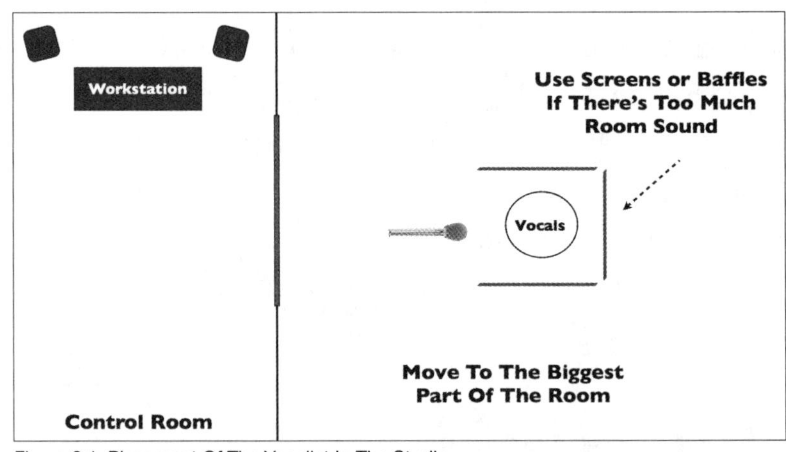

Figure 8.1: Placement Of The Vocalist In The Studio

Vocals In The Control Room

While it seems like recording blasphemy, many vocalists hate headphones and would much rather sing in the control room with a hand-held stage mic like a Shure SM58. This might not win you any hi-fidelity awards for vocal sound, but a great performance will trump audio quality any day. Plus the sound of most stage mics, while certainly not as hi-fi as a multi-thousand dollar vintage Neumann, is better than you think (as long as it's in good condition) when routed through a high-quality microphone preamp, and certainly good enough for just about any recording purpose.

Most studio mics don't work well for hand-held use because of their handling noise and the fact that singing into one with it pressed up against the singer's lips will result in a series of extreme pops and distortion. You can still make it work by wrapping the mic in some foam rubber or Sonex and putting a pop filter on the capsule head, but you're much better off to just use a tried and true stage mic and hope for the best.

Lead Vocal Mic Placement

Just like with a great sounding instrument, many times with a good singer you'll get the "sound" automatically just by putting him/her in front of the right microphone. On the other hand, with a bad or inexperienced singer, even a high priced microphone or signal processing won't add the polish you're looking for. That said, if you start with the correct technique, you're half-way there.

There are a number of things to remember before you begin to place the mic:

- The best mic in the house won't necessarily get the best vocal sounds, so don't be afraid to experiment with different mics.

- Decoupling of the stand from the floor will help get rid of many unwanted low-frequency rumbles that occur from truck traffic, machinery being used down the street, footsteps, and things that are even lower in frequency than normal hearing. Just place the stand on a couple of mouse pads or a rug for an inexpensive solution.

- One of the main things that you're trying to do with mic placement is eliminate pops, lip smacks, and breath blasts.

- An easy way to have a vocalist gauge the distance from the mic is by hand lengths. An open hand is approximately eight inches while a fist is about four inches. By saying, "Stay two fists away", the vocalist can easily judge his distance and usually doesn't forget (see Figure 8.2).

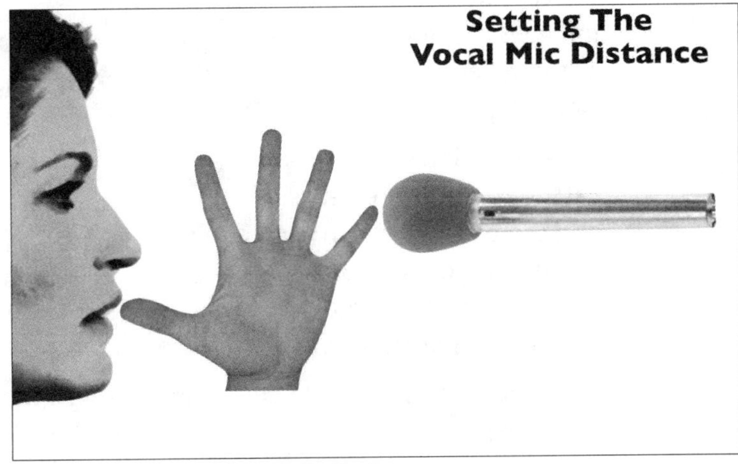

Figure 8.2: Setting Vocal Distance By Hand

Exercise Pod: Recording The Lead Vocal

E8.1: Recording Lead Vocal

A) Place the mic even with the vocalist's lips about one hand away (see Figure 8.2) and have him sing the verse of a song. Did you hear any pops or breath blasts?

B) Move the vocalist back to about two hands away and sing the same part of the song. Turn up the gain so it's the same as before. Did you hear any pops or breath blasts now?

C) Move the vocalist back to one hand away and readjust the gain. Place the mic even with the vocalist's nose and have the him sing the verse of a song. Did you hear any pops or breath blasts? Did the sound of the vocal change? Is it more or less defined?

D) Now place the mic even with the vocalist's eyes and point it down towards the lips (see Figure 8.3). Have him sing the verse of a song. Did you hear any pops or breath blasts? Did the sound of the vocal change? Is it more or less defined?

E) Now place the mic even with the vocalist's lips about one hand away again. Either change the pickup pattern to omnidirectional or change the mic to one with an omni pattern. Have him sing the verse of a song again. Did you hear any pops or breath blasts? Did the sound of the vocal change? Is it more or less defined?

F) Place the mic so there's no breath blasts or pops.

E8.2: Adding A Compressor

A) Go back to your favorite mic, place it at either nose or eye level, point at the lips, and continue.

B) Insert a compressor into the signal chain either on an insert in the console or preamp, or placed between the preamp and DAW input.

C) Set the *Attack* and *Release* controls to medium, the *Ratio* to 4:1, and raise the *Threshold* until there's 2 dB on vocal peaks. Can you hear the compressor when it kicks in? Does it change the sound of the vocal?

D) Decrease the Attack time (make it faster) until it catches more of the peaks and there's 5 or 6 dB on vocal peaks. Can you hear the compressor when it kicks in? What happens if you lengthen the Release time? Does it change the sound of the vocal?

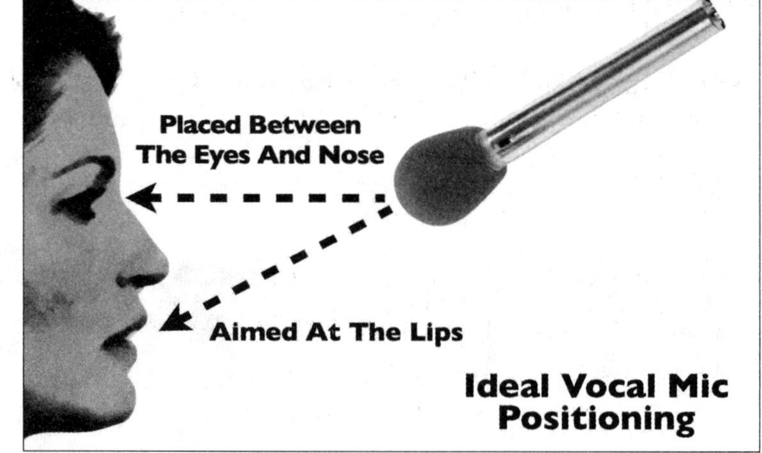

Figure 8.3: Placing The Vocal Mic

E) Set the Output control of the compressor so that the record level is about -10 dB on the meters.

You've Got To Hear Yourself

In order for a vocalist to stay in tune, she's got to hear herself. How much she hears herself will actually determine if she stays in pitch or not.

Some singers sing sharp when they're not loud enough in the headphones because they sing harder to compensate and push themselves over the top of the correct pitch. The secret is to either have more vocal or less of everything else in the monitors or phones, but be aware, pitch and timing problems also occur if a singer hears too much of the vocal and not enough of the band in the mix.

• If the vocalist is singing flat, turn him down a little or add more of everyone else in the mix. Less vocal makes you want to sing harder (and possibly raise your pitch slightly) and vice versa.

- Sometimes the mix is too dense and having a mix with fewer instruments can help with a pitch problems.

- Boost the bass guitar (the root of all chords) and kick drum (the root of all rhythm) to help the singer with pitch and staying in the pocket.

- Turn down anything that's heavily chorused and turn up anything that has a more "centered" tonal frequency (like a piano).

- Sometimes listening to only the rhythm guitar instead of two guitars (if there are two in the mix) can be helpful, since some singers can hear their pitch better from a simple tonally-centered instrument than from screaming guitars or airy synth patches.

Getting The Best From A Singer

The easiest way to get the best performance out of a singer is to make the environment comfortable. Sometimes even a seasoned pro can't do her best unless the conditions are just right, so consider some of the following suggestions before and during a vocal session.

- Ask the vocalist what kind of lighting they prefer. Most singers prefer the lights lower in the studio and the control room when performing, but ask them first.

- Adding a touch of reverb or delay to the vocal can help the singer feel more comfortable with the headphone mix.

- If you need to have the singer sing harder, louder, or more aggressively, turn down the vocal track in the phones a bit or turn the backing tracks up.

- If you need to have the singer sing softer or more intimately, turn the singer's track up in the phones or turn down the backing tracks.

- Keep talking with the artist between takes. Leave the talkback on if possible. Long periods of silence from the control room are a mood killer.

- Try lowering the lights in the control room so they can't see you. Some people think that you're in there judging them when you might be talking about something completely different.

- If the take wasn't good for whatever reason, explain what was wrong in a kind and gentle way. Something like "That was really good, but I think you can do it even better. The pitch was a little sharp." This goes for just about any overdub since players generally like to know what was wrong with the take rather than be given a "do it again" blanket statement.

- Keep smiling.

Vocal Doubling

Doubling a lead vocal has been used for as long as there's been multitrack recorders. The Beatles did it way back when they were using only 4 track magnetic tape and really didn't have a track to spare, which tells you how powerful a tool it can be.

Doubling a vocal (having the singer sing the exact same line or phrase twice and playing back both parts) works for two reasons: it makes a vocal sound stronger, and it masks any tuning inconsistencies in the part.

While the doubling technique can work for a great number of vocalists, sometimes it just doesn't sound good if both vocal tracks are replayed at the same level. Try adding the second vocal at 6 to 10 dB less than the track you deem the strongest. This will add a bit of support to an otherwise weak vocal without sounding doubled.

Recording Background Vocals

If the singer is doing all of her own background vocals, you can treat every vocal as a lead vocal, but if you have multiple vocalists to record, your approach to recording is different. Here are a few things to think about before you press the record button.

- If the lead singer is singing the background parts or is part of the background vocal ensemble, try not to use the same mic that the lead vocals were recorded on. This will cause a buildup of any peaks in the singers voice, the mic, or the room. Always try to do something a little different on each track. A different mic, mic preamp, room, singer, or distance from the mic will all help to make the sound bigger.

- If the singers have trouble blending or singing in tune, ask them to remove one side of the headphones, or at least put them slightly back on the ear. Sometimes this helps them sing in tune since they can then hear the blend acoustically.

- Large diaphragm cardioid condenser mics are usually used for background vocals because they combine a slight midrange scoop along with a slight lift in the upper frequency ranges that helps the background vocals sit better in the mix against the lead vocal.

Figure 8.4: Background Vocal Mic Placement

Background Vocal Mic Placement

The microphone placement for background vocals with multiple singers is less critical because of the extra space between the singers and mic, but the placement of the singers themselves is critical.

Exercise Pod: Recording Background Vocals

E8.3: Recording Background Vocals

A) Place a single directional mic about three feet away from the vocalists at mouth level.

B) Position the vocalists around the mic, being careful not to get them too far to the sides (since they may end up being quieter and have less definition if that happens—see Figure 8.4).

C) Set the trim and fader so the level reaches about -10 dB on the meter and have the vocalists sing their part.

D) Set the balance of the vocalists by either moving the louder ones a step backwards or the quiet ones a step forwards. Keep moving them by single step increments until the correct vocal balance is achieved.

E) When that balance is struck, mark the floor where each vocalist is standing with masking or console tape so they remember their positions.

F) Replace the directional mic with one that's omni. Can you hear any difference? Is the tone different? Is the vocal balance different?

G) Now select a different directional mic than what you started with. Can you hear any difference? Is the tone different? Is the vocal balance different?

H) Select the mic that sounds the best for the track and continue.

E8.4: Adding A Compressor To The Background Vocals

A) Insert a compressor into the signal chain either on an insert in the console or preamp, or placed between the preamp and DAW input.

B) Set the *Attack* and *Release* controls to medium, the *Ratio* to 4:1, and raise the *Threshold* until there's 2 dB on vocal peaks. Can you hear the compressor when it kicks in? Does it change the sound of the vocal?

C) Decrease the Attack time (make it faster) until it catches more of the peaks and there's 5 or 6 dB of compression on vocal peaks. Can you hear the compressor when it kicks in? What happens if you lengthen the Release time? Does it change the sound of the vocal?

D) Set the Output control of the compressor so that the record level is about -10 dB on the meters.

Placement In The Room

Besides the obvious fact that several vocalists around a mic will need more room than one vocalist would, once again it's best to move into the largest part of the studio or room to record background vocals. Since background vocals are invariably stacked, layered, or at the very least doubled, try the following to make them sound bigger and have a greater sense of space. For every subsequent overdub after the first recording, have the singers take a step backwards, but increase the mic preamp gain so that the tracks level is equal to the first track. In essence you want to "fill up the meters" so the level on the meter is the same regardless of where the singers stand.

E8.5: Recording Doubled Or Layered Background Vocals

A) After the first background vocal is recorded, record the same part a second time on a different track. Be sure that the vocalists don't move from their marked spots.

B) Pan both vocal channels to the center and play them back. Do they sound bigger than just one vocal? Do they get in the way of the lead vocal?

C) Pan both vocal channels slightly left and right and play them back. Do they sound bigger? Do they get in the way of the lead vocal now?

D) Now have each of the vocalists take one step backwards away from the mic (see Figure 8.5).

E) Have them sing the part and adjust the level so the meter reads the same as the previous vocal recording.

F) Record the next part and play back only the first and third tracks. Does it sound larger? Does it sound wider when panned? Is there more contrast with the vocal?

G) For each additional part, have the vocalists take a step backwards, and readjust the volume.

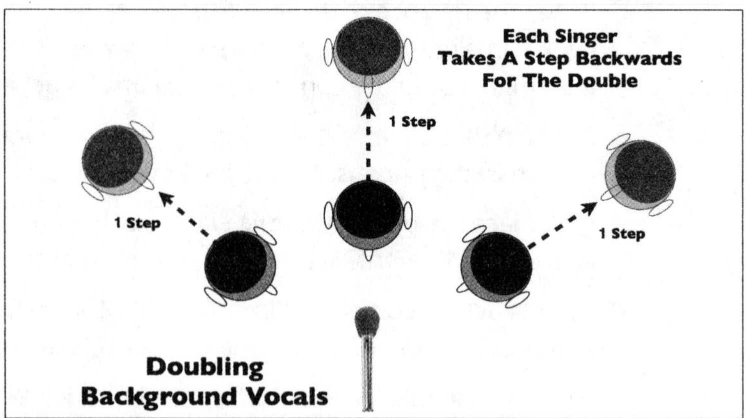

Figure 8.5: Layering Background Vocals

CHAPTER 9
RECORDING ACOUSTIC INSTRUMENTS

Regardless of the kind of acoustic instrument that you're trying to record, they all have one thing in common: they don't sound like themselves when tightly miked. Acoustic instruments need space to resonate, breathe, and project, so they don't generally respond well to extreme close-miking. While it might seem that the best place to mike the instrument is at the spot where the most sound comes out, you might find that the sound can lack definition if recorded from only that area. What you're looking for is a nice combination of high and low frequencies, but this ideal spot varies from instrument to instrument.

Finding The Right Placement In The Room

The sound of the environment makes a huge difference in the sound of the recording. If the room has a lot of flutter echo, you'll probably want less ambiance in the recording. Likewise, if the room sounds good but is too live, your recording can sound cloudy and less defined, so less ambiance is again preferred. While moving the mics a bit closer can accomplish that, you can set the player on a rug instead of the hard floor to keep the reflections to a minimum, or close off the space a little by placing baffles around the player.

Exercise Pod: Finding The Right Placement In The Room

E9.1: Finding The Right Placement In The Room

A) Set the player in the corner of the room and have him play. Note the sound. Does the low end overwhelm the sound? Can you hear the room fluttering?

B) Move the player out of the corner to the middle of the room but a few feet from a wall. Does the instrument sound any different from the corner? Can you hear any flutter or reflections from the room?

C) Now move the player out into the middle of the room equidistant from both side walls. Does the instrument sound any different from the corner? Can you hear any flutter or reflections from the room?

D) Place the player on a rug. Did the reflections diminish?

E) Place baffles around the player at a distance of about three feet. Did the reflections diminish?

F) Move the player to the best sounding part of the room and baffle as needed to cut down on the room reflections.

Acoustic Instrument Mic Placement

While there are some more or less standard ways to mic certain acoustic instruments, these are only a starting point. Remember that each recording situation is different because the player, the instrument, the room, the recording gear, the song, and the arrangement are different. That's why you can't take mic position for granted; you have to listen to the instrument first.

It's important that you go into the room with the player and listen to her play before you choose a final mic position. What's more, make sure she plays the song that you'll be recording, since scales, a warm-up, or another song won't give you a good representation of what you'll be recording, and you might get fooled as the volume or tone changes when she begins to play her part in the song you're recording.

Exercise Pod: Recording Acoustic Instruments

E9.2: Acoustic Mic Placement

A) Go out into the room as the player plays the song that you'll be recording.

B) Walk all around the player. Is there one place where the instrument sounds best?

C) Move your head back a foot. Is there a place where there's a balance between the ambiance of the room and the direct sound from the instrument? Move two feet back. Is the balance better?

D) From where you started, move your head in a foot. Is there a better balance between the ambiance of the room and the direct sound from the instrument? Move two feet in closer. Is the balance better?

E) Place the mic at the place where the instrument sounds the best and has the best balance of direct sound to room. This is a starting place. Be prepared to move the mic when you listen through the monitors and with the track.

The Acoustic Piano

The acoustic piano is one of the more difficult instruments to record well because of the extreme range of the instrument and the fact that the sound doesn't come from one place.

While placing a mic away from the piano in the room provides a great balance, that's not always possible when it's playing with other instruments, since some isolation in the recording is usually required. The problem is that when you close mic a piano, you're likely to pick up unwanted pedal and hammer sounds in addition to the music, but you'll also capture a brighter, closer sound. Here are a couple of ways to mic the piano.

Because of the transient response of the piano, condenser or ribbon mics are usually used, but don't be afraid to experiment, especially if the sound isn't working well with the other instruments in the track.

E9.3: Miking The Solo Piano

A) Have the pianist play scales. Stick your finger in one ear and walk around to find the point in the room where the hall ambiance and the direct piano sound are balanced. When you find that place, walk back and forth along the piano and listen to how the bass changes. Find a place that has the right tonality and the right balance. Place the mic there.

B) Now place a directional mic aimed at the middle of the rounded part of the piano about six feet away from the piano. Aim it at the lid. What does it sound

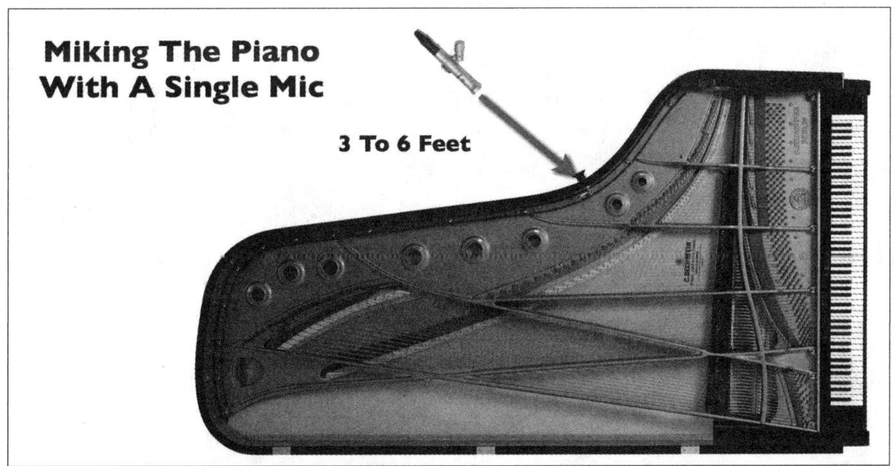

Figure 9.1: Piano Microphone Placement

like? Now aim it at the strings. What does it sound like? Is it boomy? Is there enough definition? Are there too many room reflections?

C) If there's not enough ambiance from this technique, move the mic back and up to keep the same angle (see Figure 9.1). What does it sound like? Is the sound balanced with the proper blend of low and high frequencies? Is it boomy? Is there enough definition? Are there too many room reflections?

D) Replace the mic with another directional mic. Does the sound fit the track better? Is it boomy? Is there enough definition? Are there too many room reflections?

E) Replace the mic with an omnidirectional mic. Does the sound fit the track better? Is it boomy? Is there enough definition? Are there too many room reflections?

E9.4: Close Miking The Piano

A) Place a directional mic about two feet above the center of the harp where the high and low strings cross (see Figure 9.2). Are the low and high notes balanced? Is it boomy? Is there enough definition? Are there too many room reflections?

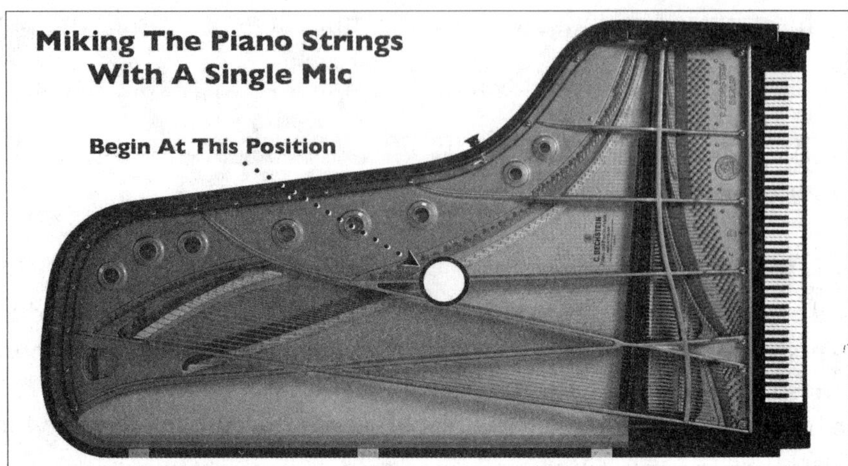

Figure 9.2: Microphone Placed Inside The Piano

B) Move the mic a foot towards the lower strings. Are the low and high notes better balanced? Is it boomy? Is there enough definition? Are there too many room reflections?

C) Move the mic a foot towards the higher strings. Are the low and high notes better balanced? Is it boomy? Is there enough definition? Are there too many room reflections?

D) Replace the mic with another directional mic. Does the sound fit the track better? Is it boomy? Is there enough definition? Are there too many room reflections?

E) Replace the mic with an omnidirectional mic. Does the sound fit the track better? Is it boomy? Is there enough definition? Are there too many room reflections?

Because of its wide range, a piano usually sounds fuller when recorded with multiple microphones in stereo. You can replace the single mic in E9.3 and E9.4 with an X/Y or ORTF pair as outlined in Chapter 11.

E9.5: Miking An Upright Piano

A) Take the panel off underneath the keyboard. Place an omnidirectional mic 12 inches away from the point where the low and high strings cross. Are the low and high notes balanced? Is it boomy? Is there enough definition? Are there too many room reflections? Can you hear foot noises on the pedals?

B) Replace the mic with a directional mic. Does the sound fit the track better? Are the low and high notes balanced? Is it boomy? Is there enough definition? Are there too many room reflections? Can you hear foot noises on the pedals?

C) Replace the mic with a different directional mic. Does the sound fit the track better? Are the low and high notes balanced? Is it boomy? Is there enough definition? Are there too many room reflections? Can you hear foot noises on the pedals?

Horns

It's pretty obvious that not all horns are created equal, and because of that, the approach to recording them isn't equal either. Then there's the fact that a horn section is recorded differently from a solo instrument, which means that we have to look at all of these recording situations separately, regardless if the section is comprised of brass or woodwinds or both.

One of the interesting things about horn players of any sort is that when they warm up, they inevitably find the spot in the room where the horn sounds best to them. Try placing the player and the mic there first, since they're already comfortable there and will play better because the room reflections seem natural.

Solo Sax

While it's natural to believe that the sound of a saxophone comes mainly from the bell, it actually comes from every hole of the instrument at the same time but in totally different proportions for every note. The bell is generally quite focused but very edgy and harsh, while the sound at the side pads generally radiate a "woody" sort of tone.

Dynamic, ribbon, and condenser mics all work well on saxes, although sometimes a ribbon can be successfully used if the sax is particularly honky since the mellowness of the ribbon combats the edginess.

Figure 9.3: Royer R-122 On Sax
(Courtesy of Roger Labs)

E9.6: Miking The Solo Sax

A) Have the sax player play the song. Place a mic about 24 inches away from the instrument about half-way up the keys, but aimed slightly down at the bell (see Figure 9.3). Can you hear every note clearly? Are certain frequencies emphasized?

B) Move the mic a six inches towards the sax. Are the low and high notes better balanced? Did the tone change? Are certain frequencies emphasized?

C) Move the mic a foot away from the sax. Are the low and high notes better balanced? Did the tone change? Are certain frequencies emphasized?

D) Move the mic over to the right side of the player, pointing in at the keys. Are the low and high notes better balanced? Did the tone change? Are certain frequencies emphasized?

E) Move the mic over to the left side of the player, pointing in at the keys. Are the low and high notes better balanced? Did the tone change? Are certain frequencies emphasized?

F) After you've found the place that sounds the best, replace the mic with another directional mic. Does the sound fit the track better? Are the low and high notes better balanced? Did the tone change? Are certain frequencies emphasized?

G) Now replace the mic with an omnidirectional mic. Does the sound fit the track better? Are the low and high notes better balanced? Did the tone change? Are certain frequencies emphasized?

I) Place the mic where the sax has the best combination of frequencies and the best balance of direct to ambient sound.

Solo Brass Instrument

Most brass instruments are edgy and benefit greatly from the mellowness of a ribbon mic, but once again, placement is a major concern. If the mic is aimed directly at the bell from a close distance, every bit of spit, excess tongue noise, air leak, and all the other nasties that every brass player occasionally produces are much more apparent. Pointing the mic a little off axis of the bell can hide the majority of these unwanted extraneous noises without compromising the natural tonal color of the instrument too much, but backing the mic up a bit can result in a better tone without the noises as well.

Figure 9.4: Arturo Sandoval Playing Into A Royer R-121 (Courtesy of Roger Labs)

E9.7: Miking A Solo Brass Instrument

A) Place the mic three to four feet away, but a bit above the bell and aimed toward the mouthpiece (see Figure 9.4). Can you hear any tongue noise or air leaks? Is the sound of the instrument balanced? Are the low and high notes better balanced? Did the tone change? Are certain frequencies emphasized?

B) Move the mic six inches towards the horn. Are the low and high notes better balanced? Did the tone change?

C) Move the mic a foot away from the horn. Are the low and high notes better balanced? Did the tone change?

D) Move the mic a foot to the right side of the player. Are the low and high notes better balanced? Did the tone change?

E) Move the mic over a foot to the left side of the player. Are the low and high notes better balanced? Did the tone change?

F) After you've found the place that sounds the best, replace the mic with another directional mic. Does the sound fit the track better?

G) Now replace the mic with an omnidirectional mic. Does the sound fit the track better? Did the tone change?

H) Place the mic where the sax has the best combination of frequencies and the best balance of direct to ambient sound.

Horn Sections

Recording a horn section is a lot different from recording just a single instrument. The temptation is to place a mic on every instrument, but this may not be an effective solution since you may run out of mics or inputs, and the chances of our old nemesis phase shift returning become a lot greater. Then there's the problem of mixing all of those tracks together later as well. It's best to record a section with as few mics as possible, and it's a lot easier to do than you might think, although the approach is different in the studio than in a live performance.

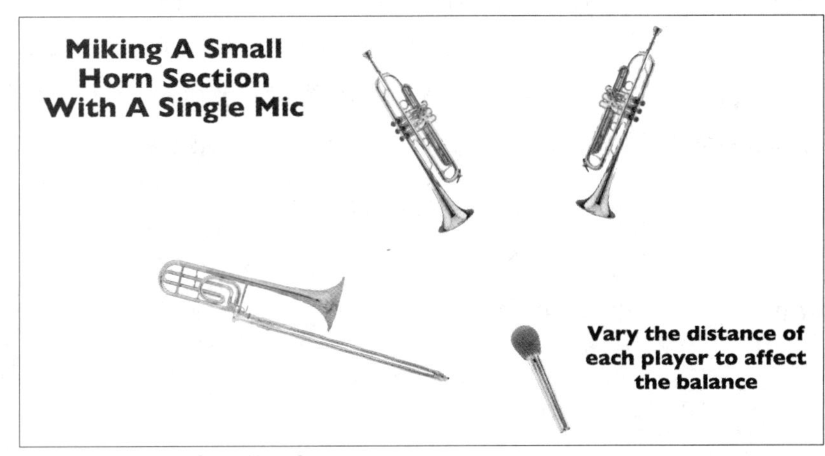

Figure 9.5: Miking A Small Horn Section

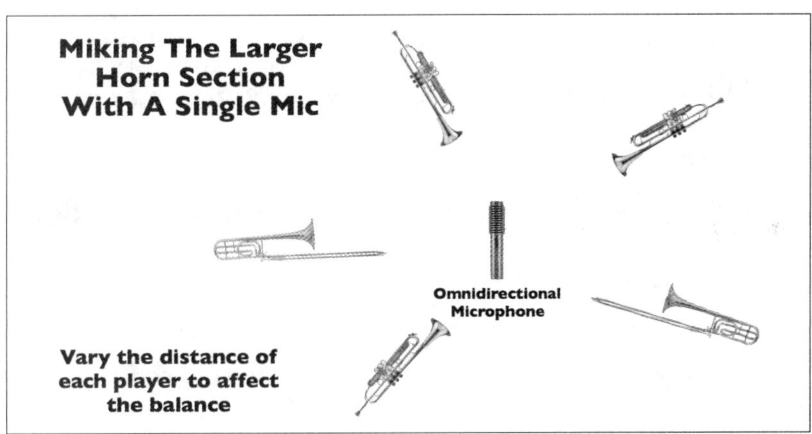

Figure 9.6: Miking A Larger Horn Section

E9.8: Miking A Horn Section In The Studio

A) For two or three players of the same family of instruments (brass instruments like trumpets and trombones, or all saxes), place the players in front of a single directional mic (see Figure 9.5). Balance the section by moving the softer horns closer to the mic and the louder ones farther away.

B) Replace the directional mic with an omni. What happened to the balance? Did the tone change?

C) If the section is more than three players, have the players positioned in a circle around an omnidirectional mic (see Figure 9.6). Balance the section by moving the softer horns closer to the mic and the louder ones farther away.

D) Replace the omni with a directional mic. What happened to the balance? Did the tone change?

E9.9: Miking A Horn Section Live Or In The Studio

A) Use a single directional mic in between every two players of the same family of instruments (brass instruments like trumpets and trombones, or all saxes). Balance the players by having them move closer or further away from the mic (see Figure 9.7).

B) Replace the mic with a different one. Did the balance change? Did the tone change?

C) Replace the directional mic with an omni. What happened to the balance? Did the tone change?

Solo String Instruments

Whether you're miking a fiddle or solo violin, viola, or cello, the approach is basically the same: get the mic further back from the instrument than you think you should because you need space to capture the sound that's projected from the instrument. Also, the closer the mic is, the more likely it'll pick up bow noise and chair movement.

All stringed instruments radiate sound omnidirectionally, but that said, brilliance of tone comes from the top of the instrument. That's why it's always better if the mic is placed where it can "see" the top of the instrument.

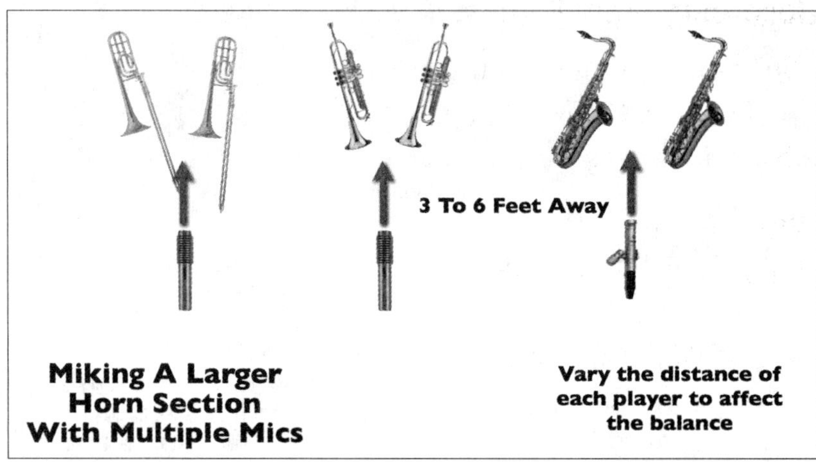

Figure 9.7: Miking A Larger Horn Section Method 2

String instruments also respond very well to condenser microphones, although ribbon mics can benefit a particularly screechy instrument.

String sections can be extremely complicated to record, so we won't touch upon it here. See *The Recording Engineer's Handbook* for more info.

E9.10: Miking A Solo String Instrument

A) Place a mic pointed at where the bow hits the strings but tilted a bit towards the neck at a distance of about 18 inches.

B) Move the mic so it's about a foot away from the instrument. Are the low and high notes better balanced? Did the tone change?

C) Move the mic so it's about six inches away from the instrument. Are the low and high notes better balanced? Did the tone change?

D) Move the mic back to where it was in A, then move it a foot to the right side of the player. Are the low and high notes better balanced? Did the tone change?

E) Move the mic over a foot to the left side of the player. Are the low and high notes better balanced? Did the tone change?

F) After you've found the place that sounds the best, replace the mic with another directional mic. Does the sound fit the track better?

G) Now replace the mic with an omnidirectional mic. Does the sound fit the track better?

H) Put a finger in your ear and walk around the instrument. Does it sound better in a different place? Where does it sound the best in terms of tone?

I) Place the mic where the instrument has the best combination of frequencies and the best balance of direct to ambient sound.

Percussion

There are two types of percussion: drum-style percussion like congas and bongos, and hand-held percussion like shakers, tambourines, and triangles. Because they're so different, they each require a different approach.

Recording Drum Percussion

For drum percussion, it's important that they're tuned first. See Chapter 6 on drum tuning, and use the same technique. It's also important to have a good sounding room with a hard floor for the best sound.

While dynamic mics are sometimes used, in order to capture the transients of the instrument condenser mics are preferred because of their quick reaction time.

E9.11: Recording Drum Percussion

A) Using a single mic, place it about 12 inches over the drum, aimed towards the middle of the head (see Figure 9.8). For two drums like congas, place the mic between the drums but aim it slightly towards the drum that's tuned higher. Does the sound have enough body? Is there too much or not enough room ambiance?

B) Aim the mic more towards the rim of the drum. What happens to the tone? Can you hear the hand slap better or worse?

C) Lower the mic to about 6 inches above the drum. What happens to the tone? Can you hear the hand slap better or worse?

Figure 9.8: Miking Drum Percussion

D) Raise the mic to about 18 inches above the drum. What happens to the tone? Can you hear the hand slap better or worse? Does the sound have enough body? Is there too much or not enough room ambiance?

E) After you've found the place that sounds the best, replace the mic with another directional mic. Does the sound fit the track better? Did the sound change? Does the sound have enough body? Is there too much or not enough room ambiance?

F) Now replace the mic with an omnidirectional mic. Does the sound fit the track better? Did the sound change? Does the sound have enough body? Is there too much or not enough room ambiance?

G) Put a finger in your ear and walk around the instrument. Is there a place where it sounds better?

H) Place the mic where the drum has the best combination of frequencies and the best balance of direct to ambient sound.

Recording Hand-Held Percussion

Hand-held percussion like shakers and tambourines have become a big part of the rhythm section as they're responsible for adding motion to the song. There's a number of things to consider when recording them though. First, the instrument must be moved when playing, so close-miking usually won't work. And second, the transient response of most hand-held instruments puts added strain on the entire signal chain, so it's always best to record with extra headroom.

Because of the transient response, ribbon and condenser mics are normally used since they have a response fast enough to capture those short energy bursts.

E9.12: Recording Hand-Held Percussion

A) Place a condenser mic set to an omni pattern about five feet away at about head level, but pointing down at the instrument (see Figure 9.9). Make sure the level of the DAW is about at -10dB on peaks. Does the instrument sound clean or is it distorted? Can you hear much of the room ambiance?

B) Move the mic so it's about two feet away. Did the tone change? What happened to the input of the mic amp or DAW? Does the instrument sound clean or is it distorted? Can you hear much of the room ambiance?

C) Move the mic back to about five feet away. Change the mic to a directional pattern. Did the tone change? What happened to the input of the mic amp or DAW? Does the instrument sound clean or is it distorted? Can you hear much of the room ambiance?

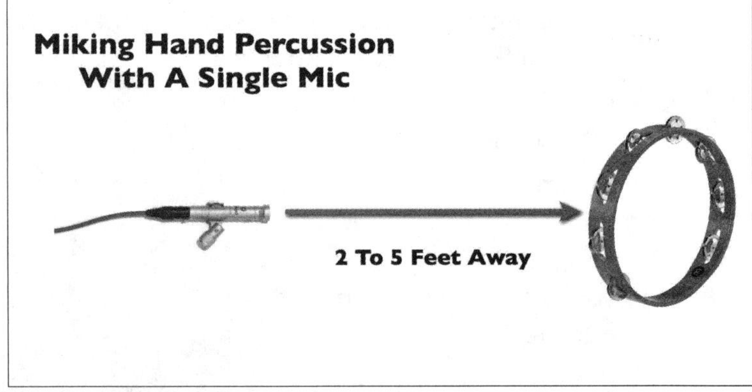

Figure 9.9: Miking Hand Percussion

D) Increase the level of the mic amp so that the meter on the DAW reads as close to zero as possible. Did the tone change? Does the instrument sound clean or is it distorted? Can you hear much of the room ambiance?

H) Return the mic amp level so it reads about -10 dB on peaks, and place the mic where the the shaker has the best combination of frequencies and the best balance of direct to ambient sound.

Other Acoustic Instruments

If you need to record an acoustic instrument that hasn't been covered here, don't worry, just follow these steps.

- **Listen to the instrument.** Just stand and listen to the instrument play for a few minutes. Get a good feel for how the instrument really sounds so you can compare it to the recording when you hear it played back.

- **Listen to the room.** Listen to how the instrument resonates in the room you're playing in. Does it enhance the instrument's sound or detract from it?

- **Find the sweet spot.** Listen for the spot that has the best balance of tone and ambiance. That's where to place the mic first, but adjust from there.

- **Move the mic instead of EQing.** Sometimes you can accomplish a lot more quicker and easier by just moving the mic a few inches either way instead of reaching for the signal processing. Not only that, it will sound more natural as well.

- **Change the mic instead of EQing.** Sometimes changing to a different mic can make an instrument fit into the mix better. It will sound more natural than adding signal processing.

CHAPTER 10
RECORDING ELECTRONIC INSTRUMENTS

Recording electronic instruments is essentially the same as recording the guitar or bass direct as covered in Chapter 7, but with a few twists and variations.

Recording Electronic Keyboards

Many keyboards have lush stereo sounds (like grand pianos) that sound great—by themselves. The trouble is that many of these sounds are made stereo artificially with a chorus effect, which doesn't always translate well when mixed together with other instruments. What's worse is that if you use the keyboard's "L/mono" output, a lot of the sounds start to sound really thin and cheesy. If this happens, try using your keyboard's "other" output if it has one. That's the one that doesn't give you one side of the stereo picture, but won't have two out-of-phase piano samples thinning out the sound. If you don't have an "other" output available, many new keyboards also have piano sounds optimized for mono, which will sound better than just one side of stereo or the stereo blended into mono.

While a few electronic keyboards now come with a low impedance XLR connection that allows you to just connect a standard mic cable, most still require you to use either a direct box (or two for stereo) or the Hi-Z/Instrument inputs on your console or preamp.

E10.1: Recording Electronic Keyboards

A) After you've plugged the keyboard into the direct box and the output of the box into a console, mic preamp, or DAW, flip the ground switch to find the quietest setting.

B) Set the levels so the peaks never go beyond -6 dB and generally stay around -10 dB.

C) Plug a compressor either into the output of the mic preamp, or an insert on the console. Start with the compressor set to either a 4:1 or 8:1 compression ratio, with both the attack and release controls set to medium.

D) Set the *Threshold* control so there's at least 5 or 6 dB of compression happening. Does it sound fuller? Did the sound change?

E) What does it sound like with 20 dB of compression? Does it sound fuller? Did the sound change?

F) Decrease both the attack and release time so they react faster. Can you hear the compressor work? Can you hear it pumping? Is the sound stronger or weaker? Did the sound change?

G) Set the level so the peaks never go beyond -6 dB and generally stay around -10 dB.

Fake Stereo

As stated above, most synthesizers and virtual instruments have a sort of pseudo-stereo effect that makes the instrument sound larger than it really is when panned hard left and right. The effect sounds great. It's big, it's wide, it's huge—all the things that an engineer loves in a mix. The problem is if you have a number of instruments that are all panned hard left and right on top of one another with the same type of effect, the result is something called "big mono."

When big mono occurs, you're not creating much of a stereo spectrum because everything is placed hard left and right, and you're robbing the track of definition and depth because all of these tracks are panned on top of one another. The solution is to throw away the track that has the warbled chorused sound, keep the dry one, and either pan in mono or just find a place to pan everything inside the extreme left and right.

E10.2: Panning Fake Stereo

A) Pan the synthesizer hard left and hard right. How does the mix sound? Can you hear the synth well or is it buried in the mix with the other instruments? What happens to the mix bus meters?

B) Pan both channels of the synth so that they're at the 10 o'clock and two o'clock positions in the stereo field. How does the mix sound? Can you hear it well or is it buried in the mix with the other instruments? What happens to the mix bus meters? Does it sound as natural?

C) Pan both channels of the synth to the center. How does the mix sound? Can you hear it well or is it buried in the mix with the other instruments? What happens to the mix bus meters? Does it sound as natural?

D) Solo each channel of the synthesizer individually and find the one that warbles, indicating that it's chorused. Now mute that channel only. Unsolo the other synth channel and listen to it in the mix. How does the mix sound? Can you hear it well or is it buried in the mix with the other instruments? What happens to the mix bus meters? Does it sound as natural?

E) Pick the sound and panning that allows you to hear the instrument clearly in the mix with other instruments.

Recording Acoustic Instruments With Pickups

Does your acoustic instrument have a built-in pickup? Many of today's acoustic instruments have either a pickup, transducer, or microphone inside. By plugging the pickup into a DI (direct injection) box, you can actually capture the sound of the instrument without using any additional microphones. This allows you to record without headphones, as the chance for feedback will be eliminated (unless the monitors are incredibly loud, and/or you have a small mic inside the guitar that picks up the speakers in the room).

Some acoustic systems, such as Fishman's popular *Blender System*, combine a mini microphone with an internal pickup (see Figure 10.1). With both mounted inside the instrument, they offer separate controls for the bass, treble, phase, and level (trim) of the acoustic output. Their *Ellipse Aura* system also features a control panel that's mounted directly on the top of the guitar, providing easy access to tone shaping. These can help create a blended and shaped tone to send directly to the mixing board.

Ultimately, an internal pickup will probably sound better if combined with a microphone. Even the best internal systems can't reproduce the full natural spectrum of an acoustic instrument, but the combination of both will also allow more options when it comes time to mix.

Using Compression

As stated before, the real secret to getting a great sounding direct recording is compression, and plenty of it. Depending upon the type of pickup that's being used, the output can be less than that of a microphone, and not as tonally balanced. That's why it's important to always use some compression to keep the sound at relatively the same level to keep the signal sounding strong and aggressive.

Figure 10.1: A Fishman Prefix Premium Blend System

Start with the compressor set to either a 4:1 or 8:1 compression ratio, with both the attack and release controls set to medium. Set the threshold so there's about 5 or 6 dB of compression happening. Depending upon the type of rhythm that you're playing, you may want to decrease both the attack and release time so they react faster, but be aware that the sound will begin to dull if the attack is too fast, and you'll begin to hear the compressor work if the release time is too short.

E10.3: Recording Acoustic Instruments With Pickups

A) After you've plugged the instrument into the direct box and the output of the box into a console, mic preamp, or DAW, flip the ground switch to find the quietest setting.

B) Set the levels so the level stays around -10 dB.

C) Plug a compressor either into the output of the mic preamp, or an insert on the console. Start with the compressor set to either a 4:1 or 8:1 compression ratio, with both the attack and release controls set to medium.

D) Set the *Threshold* control so there's at least 5 or 6 dB of compression happening. Does it sound fuller? Does it still sound wimpy?

E) What does it sound like with 20 dB of compression? Does the instrument sound fuller? Does it still sound wimpy?

F) Decrease both the attack and release time so they react faster. Can you hear the compressor work? Can you hear it pumping? Is the sound stronger or weaker?

The Acoustic Preamp/DI

Some companies make DIs specifically for the acoustic guitar, but they can be successfully used to record other kind of acoustic instruments as well. The popular LR Baggs *Para Acoustic* DI combines a direct box with a preamp and a 5-band equalizer. It includes such features as phase inversion, an effects loop, and a balanced XLR output. LR Baggs *Venue DI* direct box model also includes a tuner and Mute and Boost footswitch (see Figure 10.2).

Fishman's *Pro EQ Platinum Acoustic Preamp* also handles the same duties, plus it includes a ground lift, 5-band EQ, phase switch, and 1/4" and XLR output capabilities. Taking it a step further, TC Electronic's *G-Natural Multi Effects Processor* for acoustic guitar features programmable delays, reverbs, compression, boost, and more, but it also includes a mic input (for either guitar or vocal), allowing you to combine a DI and mic signal in one unit.

Any of these types of pedals/DIs can be used both onstage and in the studio if your instrument has an internal pickup with a 1/4" or XLR output. In the studio, you could run the XLR signal from the pedal's output directly into a recording channel and combine it with a mic for further tonal options.

Figure 10.2: LR Baggs Venue DI Direct Box

Combined With An Amp

If your acoustic instrument does have a pickup, you might also consider running the signal into an amp instead of into a DI, and miking the amp along with the instrument. This can provide two distinct sounds to work with: the natural acoustic sound and that of the amplified signal. You could also choose to just mic up the amplifier and leave the instrument un-miked for a less traditional acoustic sound.

This technique is especially effective when running the acoustic instrument into amplifiers that have a nice deep reverb or a vibrato or tremolo effect. These effects, along with the overdrive that an amp can supply, provide a sound that can't be easily duplicated by amp simulators or effects. Some interesting results can be achieved by letting the amp sound "bleed" into the acoustic mic, creating its own natural blend. Follow the miking techniques for amps from Chapter 7.

CHAPTER 11
RECORDING IN STEREO

Until now we've talked entirely about miking an instrument in mono, but almost all instruments, especially acoustic instruments and ensembles, can benefit greatly from stereo miking. Stereo miking is when you use two mics in a particular configuration to record an instrument in order to get a larger, more realistic soundfield. Stereo recording provides a sense of the soundfield from left to right and a sense of depth or distance between each instrument that you just can't get with mono miking.

Even if you never intend to record an ensemble larger than a standard rhythm section, a good grasp on the many techniques for stereo recording will come in handy sooner or later. Stereo miking is commonly used when recording drum kits, pianos, string sections, organ Leslies, and the like, and can certainly be applied to just about any recording situation.

There are a lot more stereo miking techniques than you'd think, but these are the ones that are most commonly used.

The X/Y Configuration

The X/Y configuration is perhaps the easiest to set up and mostly widely used stereo configuration. It requires two identical directional microphones that are mounted so that their grilles are nearly touching, but with their diaphragms angled apart in such a way that they aim approximately toward the left and right sides of the instrument or ensemble.

Unlike what you may think, the mics are not crossed in an X pattern in this configuration. In fact, the mic capsules are placed as close as possible to one another in a 90° angle (see Figure 11.1). The greater the angle between microphones, and the narrower the polar pattern, the wider the stereo spread.

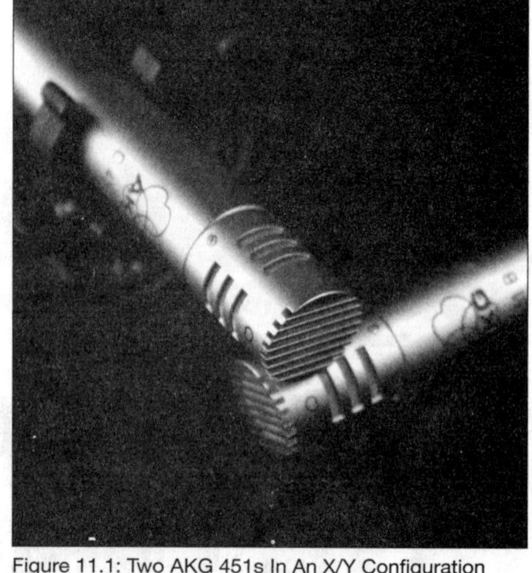

Figure 11.1: Two AKG 451s In An X/Y Configuration

Exercise Pod: Recording In Stereo

E11.1: Recording In X/Y

A) Walk around the room and listen to where the instrument or sound source sounds best. Note the instrument-to-room balance and the stereo image.

B) Set up two identical cardioid mics in an X/Y configuration where the middle of your head was.

C) Set the *Trim* or *Gain* controls and fader levels so both mics are at the same level. Now pan the channels hard left and hard right. How does it sound?

D) Replace one of the mics with a different cardioid model. How does it sound? Is one side brighter or more bassy than the other? Did the stereo image move?

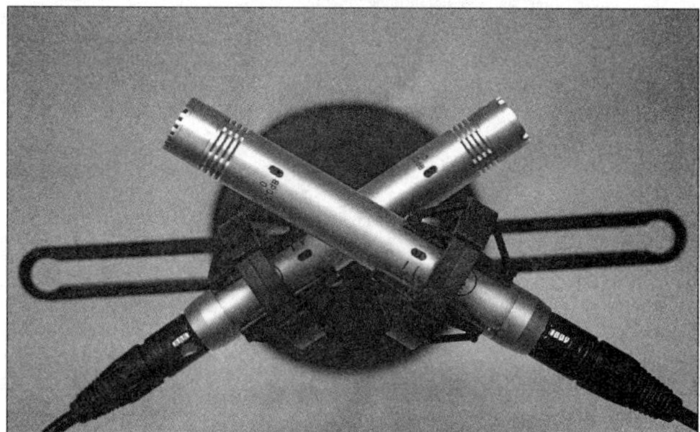

Figure 11.2: An ORTF Configuration

E) Return to the configuration with the identical mics. Change the angle of the mics from 90 to 60°. How does it sound? Is the stereo image wider or narrower? Did the stereo image move?

F) Change the angle of the mics from 60 to around 120°. How does it sound? Is the stereo image wider or narrower? Did the stereo image move?

G) Pan both mic channels to the center. What does it sound like now? Does it sound hollow? Are there any frequencies missing?

H) Return the configuration to 90° and pan both mic channels to mono. How does it sound now?

The ORTF Configuration

The most common example of stereo miking is the ORTF system, which uses two cardioids angled 110° apart and spaced seven inches apart horizontally (ORTF stands for Office de Radiodifusion Television Française, or the Office of French Radio and Television Broadcasting). This method tends to sound very accurate since the microphone capsules are as far apart as your ears (see Figure 11.2).

E11.3: Recording In ORTF

A) Walk around the room and listen to where the instrument or sound source sounds best. Note the instrument-to-room balance and the stereo image.

B) Set up two identical cardioid mics in an ORTF configuration where the middle of your head was.

C) Set the *Trim* or *Gain* controls and fader levels so both mics are at the same level. Now pan the channels hard left and hard right. How does it sound?

D) Replace one of the mics with a different cardioid model. How does it sound? Is one side brighter or more bassy than the other? Is one side louder than the other? Did the stereo image move?

E) Return to the configuration with the identical mics. Move the mics two feet closer to the source. Is the stereo image wider or more narrow? Can you hear more or less of the room?

F) Return the configuration to the distance that you started with. Now move it three feet further away. Is the stereo image wider or more narrow? Can you hear more or less of the room?

G) Pan both mic channels to the center. What does it sound like now? Does it seem like any frequencies are missing?

Figure 11.3: A On-Stage MY700 Stereo Bar

Stereo Accessories

Setting up an X/Y or ORTF stereo miking configuration can be a real pain, since it requires a couple of heavy duty mic stands and a lot of patience to place everything just right. If you're planning on doing a lot of stereo miking, a worthwhile purchase is a stereo bar (see Figure 11.3). This allows you to use just one mic stand and allows for precision placement of a couple of mics in any configuration. They're made by a variety of manufacturers like AKG, Shure, Sabra, Rycote, K&M, and On Stage Stands.

The Spaced Pair

With the spaced-pair technique, two identical mics are placed several feet apart, aiming straight ahead toward the instrument or musical ensemble. The mics can have any polar pattern, but the omnidirectional pattern is the most popular for this method. The greater

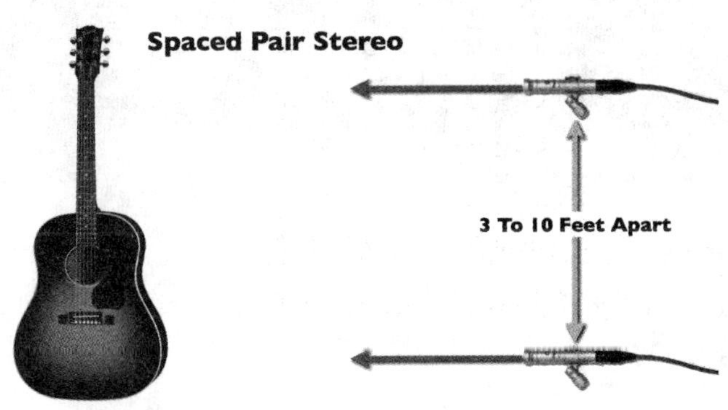

Figure 11.4: Spaced Pair Diagram

the spacing between mics, the greater the stereo spread (see Figure 11.4), although the normal spacing is usually somewhere between 3 and 10 feet.

This may seem like such a simple setup, but getting the spacing right is actually pretty difficult. If the spacing between mics is too far apart, the stereo separation seems exaggerated. On the other hand, if the mics are too close together, there will be an inadequate stereo spread. In addition, the mics will tend to favor the center of the ensemble because the mics are closest to the center instruments.

E11.2: Recording With A Spaced Pair

A) Set up two identical mics about three feet away from the instrument or ensemble and nine feet apart. Make sure that the instrument or ensemble is in the middle of the two mics.

B) Bring up the level of both mics so they're identical, pan them hard left and hard right, have the player or players play, and listen. What does the stereo spread sound like?

C) Pan each channel to the center. Have any frequencies disappeared? Does it sound natural?

D) Return the panning to hard left and right. Now move the mics closer together together so they're four feet apart. What does the stereo spread sound like now? Is it wider or more narrow? Have any frequencies disappeared? Does it sound natural?

E) Now move the mics so they're about six feet apart. What does the stereo spread sound like now? Is it wider or more narrow? Have any frequencies disappeared? Does it sound natural?

F) Now move the mics back so they're about six feet from the source. What does the stereo spread sound like now? Is it wider or more narrow? Have any frequencies disappeared? Does it sound natural? Is there more ambiance?

Using A Stereo Mic

A stereo mic takes all the worry out of mic placement since the capsules are permanently fixed within a single housing (see Figure 11.5). It's a quick and easy way to put together a stereo setup since only one mic stand is required.

Figure 11.5: Royer SF-12 Stereo Microphone
Courtesy of Royer Labs

Stereo mics tend to be mostly condensers since the capsules can be made small enough to fit together inside a body. There are a few stereo ribbon mics, but stereo dynamic mics are rare.

E11.4: Recording With A Stereo Mic

A) Walk around the room and listen to where the instrument or sound source sounds best. Note the instrument-to-room balance and the stereo image.

B) Set up the stereo mic in that spot.

C) Set the *Trim* or *Gain* controls and fader levels so both outputs of the mic are at the same level. Now pan the channels hard left and hard right. How does it sound?

D) Move the mic in a foot closer. What does the stereo image sound like? Is it bigger or smaller sounding? Move in another foot closer. What does it sound like now?

E) Return the mic to its original position. Now move the mic a foot further away. What does the stereo image sound like? Is it bigger or smaller sounding? Move another foot further away. What does it sound like now?

F) Now pan the channels to the 9 and 3 o'clock positions. What is the soundfield like? Is the sound more or less focused?

G) Now pan the channels to the 11 and 1 o'clock positions. What is the soundfield like? Is the sound more or less focused?

CHAPTER 12
THE RECORDING SESSION

Recording sessions are broken down into two types: tracking sessions in which the basic tracks are recorded, and overdub sessions where instruments or vocals from the basic track are replaced with better versions or additional instruments or vocals are layered on top. Although in both cases you're just trying to record some musicians playing, the recording mindset for each is different.

The Basic Track

Basic tracks, or "basics," are the initial recording of the rhythm section prior to any overdubs or sweetening. Basic tracks are the foundation for the music being recorded and any other parts that come afterward, so if there's something faulty in the recording, it's usually going to cost time and money to fix later. That's why it's essential that the basic track recording is as good as it can be both sound and quality-wise.

Basic tracks can consist of any of the following instruments, depending upon the song, artist, project, or genre of music:

- The drums by themselves
- Drums and bass
- Drums, bass, and guitar
- Drums, bass, and keyboard
- Drums, bass, guitar, and keyboard
- The entire band, regardless of how many instruments

Any of the above may be accompanied by a vocalist singing a "scratch" vocal, which is used as a guide so the players know where they are in the song. The scratch vocal is not intended to be included in the final version, although sometimes it ends up being better than anything the vocalist can do later during overdubs.

In modern basic track recording, sometimes the only thing that's intended to be kept for the final version of the song is the drums, even though other instruments are played at the same time. The theory is that if the drum track is great, everything else can be replaced as an overdub later. If that's the case, isolation of the drums becomes of paramount importance, since any leakage of other instruments like a guitar or bass may clash with later overdubs.

That being said, most veteran producers would prefer to get a great basic recording with as many instruments as possible at the same time, since the elusive "vibe" of all the players playing together usually can't be duplicated any other way.

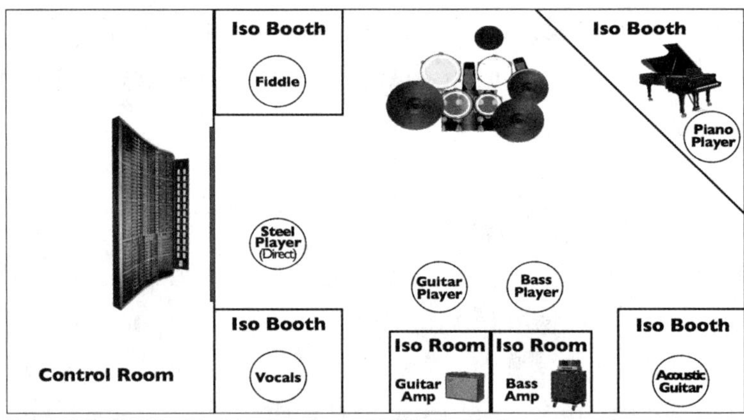

Figure 12.1: A Typical Rhythm Section Tracking Session In A Major Studio

Setup

While many modern recordings are made with as few players as possible playing at once, most recording veterans prefer to have as many players as possible during the basic tracking date. The reasons? The vibe and the sound. While such a session can be rather nerve-wracking in complexity for the engineer, it can be a lot of fun as well. Figure 12.1 shows a diagram of a typical tracking session of a four piece band and a singer in a major recording studio. Note the isolation rooms for the vocals and amps.

Nashville is still one of the last places where a typical tracking

Figure 12.2: A Typical Tracking Session In A Nashville Studio

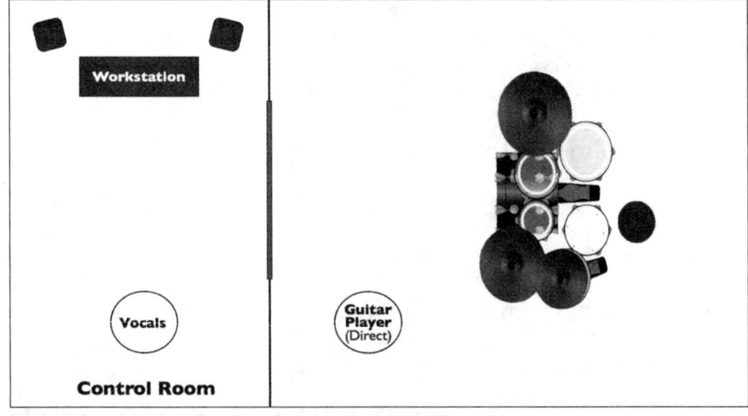

Figure 12.3: A Typical Tracking Session In A Home Studio

date can involve a lot more people than just a rhythm section. In the scenario in Figure 12.2, there are seven players plus a vocalist.

Most of us don't have the luxury of a large studio with lots of iso rooms, so the basic tracking session becomes a lot more modest. Figure 12.3 shows a typical scenario in a small home recording studio with only the drums, guitar, and vocal being recorded with the hopes of just getting a keeper drum track.

For a multi-day session, the first day of tracking is also setup day. Usually it takes about a half-day for everyone to feel comfortable, for the engineer to get sounds, and for the musicians to get their headphone mixes together. Somewhere during the second half of the day is when the band begins recording.

For a budget session where you only have a single day to record, you want to get set up and recording as soon as possible, certainly within the first hour after the musicians arrive. The best way to do this is to be sure of all the details of the session, such as how many players there will be, whether there will be more than one singer, whether the band is bringing their own disc drive, what recording format they prefer, and any additional gear expected. If the studio is already set up by the time the band arrives, the time it takes to get recording will be cut to a minimum.

Where To Place The Players In The Room

Regardless of how good the headphone system is, the players won't play their best unless they can see each other, so that becomes priority number one (see Figure 12.4). Even if the players know a song down cold, they can't react to any nuances without clean sight lines to each other. Plus, many players (especially studio veterans) rely on looking at the drummer playing the snare in order to stay locked in time.

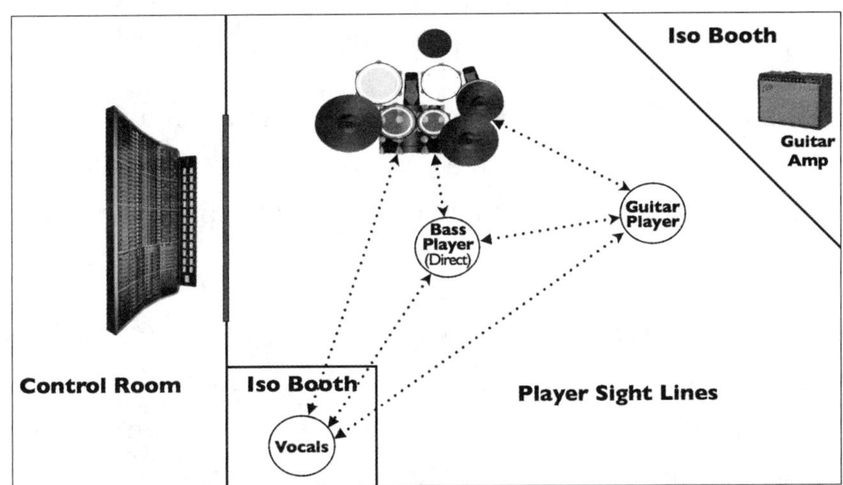

Figure 12.4: Player Sight Lines Are Important

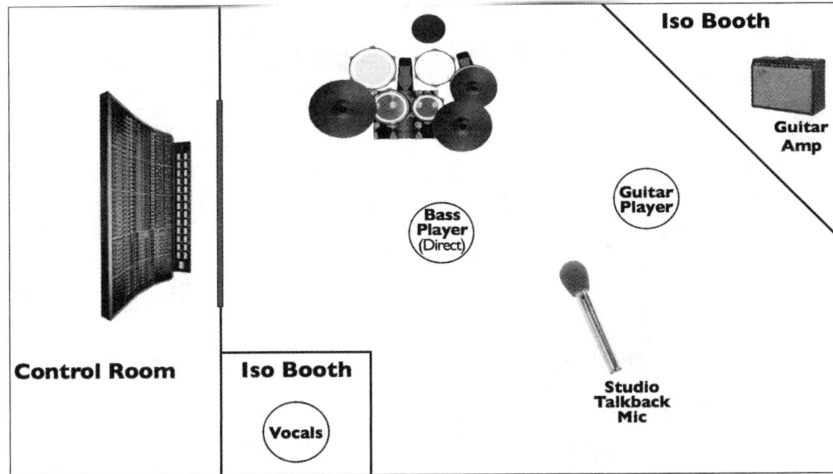

Figure 12.5: The Studio Talkback Mic

The Talkback Mic

Before tracking it's important to put at least one talkback mic as close to the middle of the tracking room as possible, even if some of the musicians are recording in a separate iso booth (see Figure 12.5). This is so you can hear them talking to you in between takes. While you can hear the players talk over the open mics (especially the drum mics), it's usually not loud enough and you don't want to have to boost the level of any of the channels and destroy your settings in an effort to hear what someone is saying to you. Adding a dedicated talkback mic (or even two in a large studio) will make it a lot easier to hear what everyone has to say after each take. Just make sure to mute it when the band is playing as it will sound tremendously trashy and distorted, since it's set up for people talking and not playing.

Leakage

Acoustic spill (known as leakage) from one instrument into another's mic is many times thought of as undesirable, but can and should be used to enhance the sound instead of avoided. Many recording novices are under the mistaken belief that during a tracking session with multiple instruments, every track recorded must contain only the instrument/source that the mic was pointed at. Since that's pretty hard to achieve, why not just use the leakage to embellish the tracks instead?

Instead of trying to avoid the leakage, great attention should be given to *the kind of leakage* being recorded rather than trying to eliminate it. Leakage can be used as a sort of glue between instruments in much the same way that instruments magnify one another in a live situation.

So, when tracking multiple instruments, try keeping the players and their gear as close together as possible (see Figure 12.6). Not only will it help the players communicate, but the leakage will be more direct sound than room reflections, which will make it sound better. This might make overdubs clash with the basic tracks, so it's best to have keeper tracks from all the instruments to get the desired effect. Of course, if you can completely isolate things like guitar and bass amps in another room, all the better.

The Headphone Mix

The keys to great basic tracks are the focus of

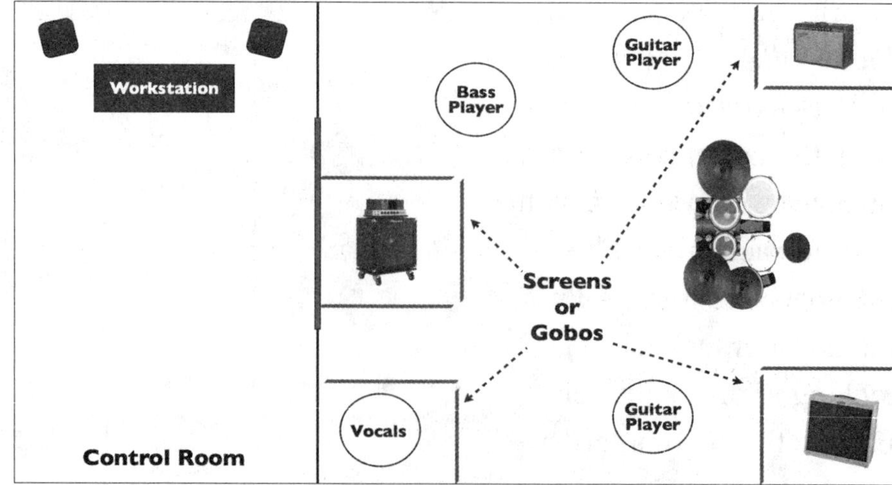

Figure 12.6: Setting Up To Take Advantage Of Leakage

the participants and the comfort of the players. Although the environmental comforts are helpful, a player will play or sing her best when she hears herself well and in the correct proportion to the other players or singers. That's why the headphone (sometimes called "cue") mix is so important.

Perhaps the greatest detriment to a session running smoothly is when players can't hear themselves comfortably in the headphones. This is one of the reasons that veteran engineers spend so much time and attention to the cue mix and the phones themselves. In fact, a sure sign of a studio neophyte is treating the headphones and cue mix as an afterthought, instead of spending as much time as required to make them sound great. While it's true that a veteran studio player can shrug off a bad or distorted phone mix and still deliver a fine performance, good "cans" makes a session go a lot faster and easier.

Make sure that you use the best headphones possible, and that they're not broken or intermittent. Nothing stops a session quicker than a player with a headphone problem.

Setting Up The Headphone Mix

The headphone mix comes from one or two of the aux sends on either your mixer, interface, or DAW (see Figure 12.7); a mono mix uses a single aux send while a stereo mix uses two (if a stereo aux isn't available). It's the same as setting up a mix using the faders, except you're using the sends instead. It's best to stay away from the sends in the DAW app because it will sound a bit delayed because of the latency involved (the time it takes for the computer to process the audio). That's why most audio interfaces have a direct or no-latency setting for tracking, and that's what you should use (see the manual of your interface for more info).

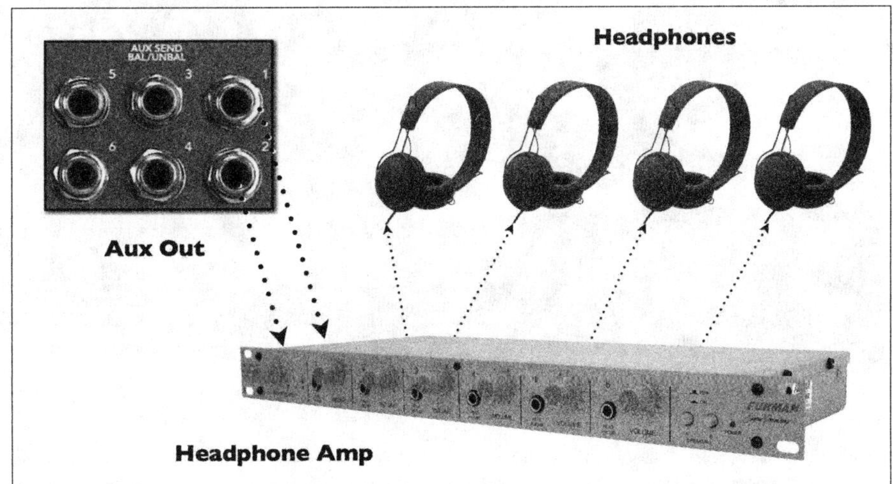

Figure 12.7: Using Aux Sends For The Cue Mix

Remember that sometimes the players don't want a balanced mix. They may want either the kick, snare, bass, a keyboard, or a vocal a lot louder than the rest of the mix to cue off of.

Exercise Pod: Basic Tracks

E12.1: Setting Up A Headphone Mix

A) Select an aux send or sends that you'll use for your headphone mix. Connect the output of the buses to a headphone amp.

B) While listening on a set of phones, listen to the mix either from the DAW or live, and raise the level of the aux send for each instrument until you have a representative mix in the phones.

C) Have the players run down the song. Ask them what they need more or less of in the mix and adjust accordingly.

Personal Headphone Mixes

Perhaps the best thing to come along in recent years has been the introduction of the relatively inexpensive personal cue mix systems. These systems allow the musician to control the headphone mix by supplying him with up to 8 channels to control. Each headphone mixer/box also contains a headphone amplifier that can (depending upon the product) provide earsplitting level. Manufacturers include Furman, Oz Audio, Aviom, and Hear Technologies (see Figure 12.8), among others.

A personal mixer doesn't require you to set up a mix for the player, just to supply him with the individual track sends. Even though that's the case, it's best to provide a stereo monitor mix (what you're listening to in the control room) as well as the kick, snare, vocal, and whatever other instruments are pertinent so that the player can mix it the way he feels comfortable. The stereo mix that you provide acts as the main mix, and the other tracks enable him to boost that element as needed.

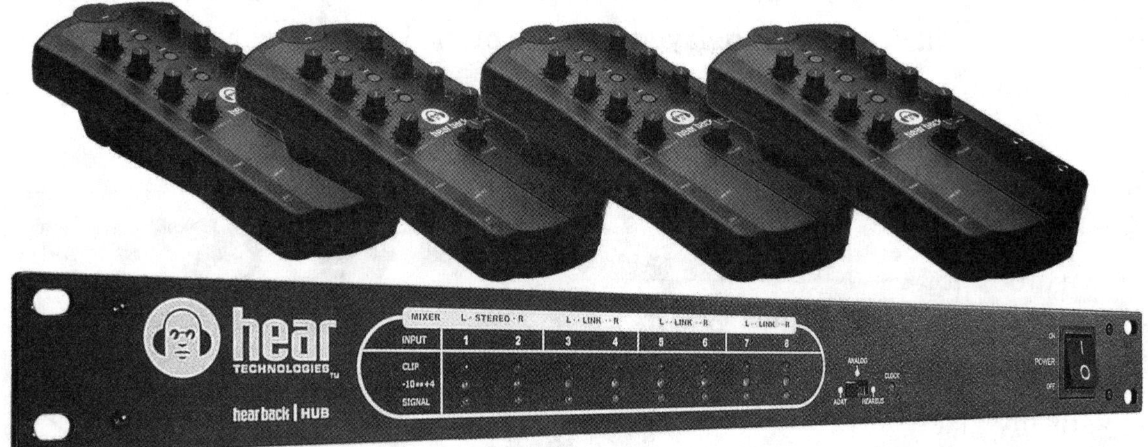

Figure 12.8: Hearback Headphone System

E12.2: Setting Up A Headphone Mix Using A Personal Mixer

A) Select the tracks that the musicians want for their headphone mix. This might be the kick, snare, bass, vocal, guitars, keyboards, and sometimes the stereo mix that you're listening to in the control room.

B) Connect each direct output to the input of the distribution system.

C) Have the players run down the song so they can adjust their own mixes.

E12.3: Basic Track Setup

A) As discussed in Chapter 6, find the best sounding part of the room and place the drums there.

B) Place any other players on the session as close to the drums as possible. If they can't be near the drums, make sure they can easily see both the arms and legs of the drummer if possible.

C) Place the mics as indicated previously in the book. Make sure they're all tested and they work properly.

D) Set headphones out for each player. Make sure they're all tested and they work properly.

E) Begin getting sounds starting with the drummer as per Chapter 6. Make sure the drummer can hear himself in the headphones and can hear your talkback to him.

F) Go one by one to each player on the session and test their mic or direct, make sure that they can hear themselves in the phones, and that they can hear your talkback.

G) Make sure that you can hear everyone in the studio on the studio talkback mic that you set up. Adjust the gain so everyone can be heard.

H) Turn off the studio talkback mic and have the band play a verse and chorus of the song they're about to record so they can gauge the headphone mix. Make sure you record it.

I) Ask the musicians for feedback to improve the headphone mix.

J) Play the song back so they can adjust their headphone mixes if they have personal mix boxes, or adjust the cue sends if you're controlling them.

K) Repeat until the musicians are comfortable with their mix. You're now ready to record.

Recording Without Headphones

Many bands are so used to playing live on stage that they just can't get used to headphones. Here's a way that allows them to get what they need while recording without having to put tiny speakers on their heads.

- The key to not using headphones in a spread out recording situation is to get the players sitting or standing close to the drums. The visual of everyone that close together helps to minimize the acoustic delay times that occur when you spread the players out too far.

- If there are two guitar players, set them up on opposite sides of the kit. This will provide a better stereo picture for the leakage.

- At times, a floor monitor (like at a gig) will work well for scratch vocals. Sometimes if you're trying to place the singer in the same room with the band, you'll get a better performance. Just like the guitar and bass amps, you may need to move it around for balance.

- Most of the time the singer will actually gravitate to the spot in the room where the band's balance is best.

The Click Track

The click track, or recording while listening to a metronome in the headphones, has become a fact of life in most recording sessions these days. Not only does playing at an even tempo sound better, but it makes cut and paste editing between different performances in a DAW possible and easy. Having a track based on a click also makes things like delay and reverb timing easier during the mix.

Playing to a click can present a number of problems, however, like leakage of the click into the mics, or the fact that some people just can't play on time to save their lives.

Making The Click Cut Through The Mix

Many times just providing a metronome in the phones isn't enough. What good is a click if you can't hear it, or worse yet, groove to it? Here are some tricks to make the click not only listenable, but cut through the densest mixes and seem like another instrument in the track too.

- **Pick The Right Sound.** Something that's more musical than an electronic click is better to groove to. Try either a cowbell, sidestick, or even a conga slap. Needless to say, when you pick a sound to replace the click, it should fit with the context of the song. Many drummers like two sounds for the click; something like a high go-go bell for the downbeat and a low go-go bell for the other beats or vice-versa.

- **Pick The Right Number Of Clicks Per Bar.** Some players like quarter notes while others play a lot better with eighths. Whichever it is, it will work better if there's more emphasis on the downbeat (beat 1) than on the other beats.

You'll often find a player who doesn't like to play to a click, or you'll find that they play very stiffly when listening to it. If that's the case, don't be afraid to go without one, since there's been plenty of huge hits that didn't utilize a click in the past, and no matter what anyone claims, it's not an absolute necessity. That said, in this world of drum machines, sequencers, and DAWs, most musicians today have grown used to playing with a metronome and feel comfortable with it.

Don't Forget To Record A Tuning Note

It's always a good idea to include a 10 second tuning note before each song, especially if the band isn't based around an instrument with a solid tuning that doesn't move (like a Hammond organ). This way, if for some reason the band happened to use a tuning that was a couple of cents flat, they can easily use the tuning note as their reference at a later time to get in tune. This seems like such a small thing, but you wouldn't believe how much time it can save you down the road if a situation arises where you just can't figure why everything sounds out of tune.

Don't Forget Record A Count-Off

A recorded count-off is important for those times when an overdub is required before the song starts. Even if you're playing to a click that's being generated by the DAW itself, recording the click at least four bars ahead of the downbeat is a foolproof way to make sure that any pickup or opening part is easily executed.

If a click isn't being used, it's even more important to record the count-off. Have the drummer click two bars with his drum sticks, then count, "One, (click), two, (click), one, two, three, (silent click)." Sometimes a count with the last two beats silent is used instead, like this, "One, (click), two, (click), one, two, (silent click), (silent click)." This is plenty of count for the band to get the feel, and the silent clicks on the end make it easy to edit out the count-off later without worry about clipping the downbeat.

Overdubs

Today's overdub sessions have changed a lot from when the process first became possible in the '60s. Back then, overdubbing went relatively quickly because there were very few leftover tracks to fill. Today we have almost unlimited to tracks to work with, so a whole host of production techniques like doubling and layering are available that can really make the process long and tedious. While these techniques are beyond the scope of this book (see *The Music Producer's Handbook* for more about production techniques), there are a number of points to consider before beginning overdubs.

Recording In The Control Room

Regardless of who's playing and what kind of instrument they're using, it's always best if you can get them to record in the room with you. This is easy with guitar, bass, electronic keys, and even vocals, and tougher for everything else. Having the musician able to hear exactly what you're hearing, the immediacy of communication, and the absence of headphones will usually get a much better performance out of the player.

Cables and hardware are now widely available to keep an amp in another room while the player plays in the room with you. Playing in the control room is usually not an option for more than one player at a time (which probably won't happen during overdubs anyway unless it's a horn, string, or vocal section) or with instruments that are quiet, like some percussion, acoustic guitars, or strings.

Exercise Pod: Overdubs

E12.4: Doing Overdubs In The Control Room

A) Make sure that the player can hear himself well and that the level is sufficient.

B) Bring up a mix that you feel is balanced.

C) Ask the player if he's comfortable with the balance of the mix and his overdub. Adjust as directed.

D) Proceed recording.

E) If an open mic is being used (like for a vocal), make sure that the mic is cardioid and that the player is facing the monitor speakers for maximum rejection.

F) Avoid feedback by not turning up the level too loudly.

Use The Big Part Of The Studio

If you can't overdub in the control room area, don't fall into the trap of keeping the instrument setup in the exact same place in the studio as during your basics (unless you're doing fixes to the basic tracks, where it's important to keep the setup the same). Move the vocal or instrument into the big part of the studio. All instruments sound best when there's some space for the sound to develop. You can cut down on any unwanted reflections from the room by placing baffles around the mic, the player, or singer as illustrated in Figure 8.1 in Chapter 8.

CHAPTER 13
THE ROUGH MIX

A rough mix is a quick mix. It might only take a couple of passes through the song (although it can take a lot more), but the idea is to hear how the performances just recorded work together. That's why we're less interested in the finer points of EQ and effects than the overall balance when doing a "rough." Here are some tips to get that rough mix sounding better than you thought it could.

The Quick Effects Setup

Before we begin our rough mix, let's set up some effects so we can put any instruments or vocals into an artificial space if necessary. This setup is designed to get you up and running quickly, with the parameters in a general position where they almost always sound at least acceptable, and sometimes even surprisingly good (see Figure 13.1). This setup also works well when you're tracking and need some quick effects. It uses two different reverbs and a delay.

Reverb One: This reverb will be used primarily for the drums. Set it to a "Room" with the decay at 1.5 seconds and a pre-delay of 20 milliseconds. If a High-Pass Filter is available, set it to 10kHz or even 8kHz. If a Low-Pass Filter is available, set it to 600Hz.

Reverb Two: This reverb is meant for all other instruments and vocals. Set it to a "Plate" with a 1.8 second decay time and a pre-delay of 20 milliseconds. If a High-Pass Filter is available, set it to 10kHz or even 8kHz. If a LPF is available, again set it to 600Hz.

Delay One: This delay can be used on vocals and instruments. Set it for about 220 milliseconds of delay and the feedback for a couple of repeats (about 4%).

Building The Mix

Despite what you might have heard, there is no standard instrument to start and build a mix from. Modern mixers employ various techniques and they're all valid, especially in different genres of music. For instance, here are the places from which a mix can be started:

- From the Bass
- From the Kick Drum
- From the Snare Drum
- From the Drum Overheads
- From the Lead Vocal or main instrument
- With all of the instruments and vocals in right from the beginning
- When mixing a string section, from the highest string (violin) to the lowest (bass)

Whichever way you select, remember that there's no right way or wrong way to build a mix. While different mixing methods are explored in other books like *The Audio Mixing Basic Training (AKA Boot Camp)* and *The Mixing Engineer's Handbook*, the following exercises illustrate one method that's frequently used, but feel free to change the order if it feels better to you.

Figure 13.1: The Quick Effects Setup

The Drums

Drum recording over the years has evolved from all the drums recorded on to a single track to the multiple tracks that we now use for a typical kit. Getting a drum balance in those early days was easy, since it might only have involved an overhead and kick drum mic, but today when we have from six to as many as 20 mics on a kit (sometimes recorded to that many channels), it takes a lot more work to come up with an internal drum kit balance. Because the drums play such a huge part in the drive and groove of a song, the internal mix of the drums is a very important part of virtually every modern recording.

Setting The Levels

Wherever you start your mix from, keep in mind that the master mix bus level will get louder and louder with every instrument entrance. That's why it's best to begin your mix with the mix bus meter (the master meters) reading at about -10 dB regardless of what instrument you start off with. With each instrument that enters at the same level as the current mix, the master mix meter should raise about 3 dB. Also remember that the sound of every drum will change anywhere from a little to a lot when a new drum or cymbal is added to the mix due to the leakage of the other drums into the mic.

Let's begin the mix from a typical starting place: the kick drum.

Exercise Pod: Balancing The Drums

E13.1: Building From The Kick

A) Raise the level of the kick drum until it reads about -10 dB on the master mix bus meter.

B) Raise the level of the snare until it's about the same level. Did the sound of the kick change when it was paired with the snare? Is the kick masked by the snare and no longer distinct? How high does the master mix bus meter read?

C) Go to a place in the song where there are tom fills. Raise the level of all toms until they're about the same level as the kick and snare. Did the sound of the kick and/or snare change? Does the kick and snare sound different when the toms aren't playing? How high does the master mix bus meter read?

D) Raise the level of the cymbal or overhead mics until the overall sound begins to change and the cymbals become more distinct sounding. What happened to the sound of the other drums? How high does the master mix bus meter read?

E) Raise the level of the high-hat mic until it becomes a bit more distinct sounding. Does the sound of the snare change? Does the sound of any of the toms or cymbals change? How high does the master mix bus meter read?

E13.2: Adding Effects To The Drums

A) Add a little of the reverb from Reverb One to the snare until you can just hear it. Does the drum kit sound bigger? What happens when you add more reverb?

B) If there are tom fills, add the same amount of reverb that you added to the snare to the toms. Do the toms sound bigger? What happens when you add more reverb?

C) If the high-hat is played by itself at points of the song, add a little reverb from Reverb One to put it in a space. Does it sound bigger? What happens when you add more reverb?

D) Return the reverb levels to where you can just hear it. You can add more when the other instruments are introduced into the mix.

Figure 13.2: A Channel Phase Control

Checking The Drum Phase

As stated in various parts of this book, one of the most important yet overlooked parts of a drum mix is checking the phase of the drums. This is important because not only will an out-of-phase channel suck the low end out of the mix, but it will get more difficult to fix as the mix progresses. Hopefully you've already checked the phase during recording, but it never hurts to check it again before you begin your mix.

E13.3:Checking The Drum Phase

A) With all the drums in the mix, go to the kick drum channel and change the selection of the polarity or phase control (see Figure 13.2). Is there more low end or less? Chose the selection with the most bottom end.

B) Go to the snare drum channel and change the selection of the polarity or phase control. Is there more low end or less? Chose the selection with the most bottom end.

C) Go to each tom mic channel and change the selection of the polarity or phase control. Is there more low end or less? Chose the selection with the most bottom end.

D) Go to each cymbal mic or overhead mic and change the selection of the polarity or phase control. Is there more low end or less? Chose the selection with the most bottom end.

Assigning The Drums To A Group Or Subgroup

Whenever there are two or more instrument mix elements, like a drum kit, five guitars, six background vocals, or eight percussion tracks, it's best to assign them to either a group or a subgroup in order to make any adjustments to the mix easier. The difference between a group and a subgroup is that in a group, a number of channel faders (like the drums) are electronically or digitally linked together so that if you move one fader in the group, they all move together, yet keep the same relative balance that you originally set.

A subgroup has the same effect yet works a little differently. All of the channels of the group are assigned to a subgroup fader, which is then assigned to the master mix bus. The level of all of the channels is controlled with that one fader, and if you move any fader within the group, the others don't move with it but you still change the balance of the mix. If you send to an effect or insert a compressor from the subgroup, it also affects all the instruments in that group, which can be a benefit in certain situations during mixing and is the main reason that you might choose to use a subgroup rather than a group.

E13.4: Assigning The Drum Channels To A Subgroup

A) On your console or DAW, assign all of the drum channels to a group. Move one of the faders. Do all the faders move yet keep the same balance relationship? Remove the drum channels from the group.

B) On your console or DAW, assign all of your drum channels to a subgroup. Raise or lower the subgroup fader. Does the level of the drums get louder and softer?

C) Choose the method that works best for you.

The Bass

The balance between the bass and drums is critical because it provides the power of the mix. Where once upon a time the bass amp was always miked, today most basses are taken direct, but sometimes both the amp mic and the direct signals are recorded on separate tracks as well. This might occur so that the bass sound has the best combination of bottom end and clarity.

Just like the drums, the phase between the direct bass sound and the miked one must be checked if they've both been recorded, or the bass may sound thin with no power.

Sometimes a bass that sounds a little on the small side will sound a lot fuller when combined with the kick. That's why it's important to listen to the kick and bass together before making any assessments of the final sound.

Exercise Pod: Balancing The Bass And Drums

E13.5: Check the phase between the bass amp and direct signal.

A) Raise the level of the direct signal until it reads -10 dB on the mix bus meter.

B) Mute the direct signal and raise the level of the amp signal until it also reads -10 dB on the mix bus meter.

C) Unmute the direct signal. The direct and amp signals should now be exactly the same level.

D) Change the selection of the polarity or phase control on the amp mic channel. Is there more low end or less? Chose the selection with the most bottom end.

E13.6: Balancing The Bass Channels

A) Pick whatever channel you think sounds best and raise the level so it reads -10 dB on the master mix bus meter.

B) Slowly raise the level of the second bass channel. Does the bass sound fuller and fatter? Does it sound cleare r and more distinct?

C) Set it where you think it sounds best for now. This balance will be adjusted later when more instruments are introduced into the mix.

D) Assign the bass channels to a group or subgroup.

E13.7: Balancing The Bass And Drums

A) Using your final drum mix from before, mute all the drums except the kick. It should read about -10 dB on the mix bus meter. Now mute the channel.

B) Raise the bass group or subgroup channel until the master mix bus meter reads -10 dB. Now unmute the kick drum channel. Do the kick and bass sound like they're at about the same level? What does the master mix bus meter read?

C) Unmute the other drum channels to hear the entire drum kit and the bass. Does the bass sit well with the drums? Can you hear the kick, snare, and bass distinctly?

D) Using the subtractive EQ technique from Chapter 4, sweep through the mid-frequency band until you find the offending frequency, then lower it. Do the bass and kick still clash? Are they both EQ'd at the same frequency? If so, move the frequency of one higher or lower.

E) Try using subtractive EQ on the kick instead of the bass.

The Vocals

Many mixers like to get the vocal in the mix as soon as possible, because if you wait until the end after you've mixed all the music, the balance that you've just worked on might change after the vocal is put into the mix. Plus, the vocal is usually the focal point of the song, so it's best to get that sounding great and build the song around it.

Exercise Pod: Balancing The Lead And Background Vocals

E13.8: Balancing The Lead Vocal With The Rhythm Section

A) Raise the level of the lead vocal until it's the loudest musical element. This is common in pop songs. Does the vocal overpower the rhythm section?

B) Now adjust the level of the lead vocal so it's only as loud, or even a little softer, than the bass and drums. This will emphasize the band and make the song more powerful. Can you still hear every word of the vocal?

C) Add a bit of delay to the vocal until you can just hear the effect. Does it sound bigger than before? Does it set it back in the mix and further away from the listener? What happens if you add more delay?

D) Add a bit of Reverb Two until you can just hear it. Does it sound bigger than before? Does it set it back in the mix and further away from the listener? What happens if you had more delay?

Background Vocals

Just like with the drums, an internal balance between the lead vocals and any background vocals is important to the balance of the song. With harmony vocals, the balance is crucial in order to get the correct blend and impact. Usually the highest vocal cuts pretty well, but the lowest or the one in the middle of a three part harmony gets lost. If the lowest part of the three part harmony is the melody, then it's usually the middle part that gets lost.

The easiest (but not the only) way to balance three part harmony is to begin just like you did with the rhythm section, from the bottom up. Start with the lowest vocal, add the middle vocal until the blend is such that they sound as one, then add the highest vocal part.

Make sure to assign the background vocal channels to either group or a subgroup.

E13.9: Balancing Three Part Harmony Vocals

A) With the background vocals soloed, raise the level of the lowest vocal, then the middle vocal, then the highest vocal. Do they blend so they sound like one voice?

B) Assign the background vocal channels to a group or subgroup, unsolo, and balance against the track.

C) If the lead vocal is one of the three parts, add the highest harmony vocal first and balance the two before adding the third part.

D) Add a bit of delay to the background vocal subgroup until you can just hear it. Does it sound bigger than before? Does it set it back in the mix and further away from the listener? What happens if you had more delay?

E) Add a bit of Reverb Two to the background vocal until you can just hear it. Does it sound bigger than before? Does it set it back in the mix and further away from the listener? What happens if you add more reverb?

Guitars

Guitars can make up every type of arrangement element, depending strictly upon the song. They can be part of the rhythm section, playing quarter note chords with the snare drum; they can play big power chords that act as the pad element of the song; or they can strum in double time to push the song along as the rhythm element. If that isn't enough, they can be the lead instrument in solos; be intros; be the lead in an instrumental; or be fills, playing in the holes around the vocal.

Often multiple guitar tracks are layered to achieve a bigger sound, which can cause problems that can't always be taken care of by balance alone. Some frequency adjustment of the tracks, which we covered in Chapter 4, is required to keep them from fighting each other.

Exercise Pod: Balancing Guitars

E13.10: Balancing Guitars

A) Raise the level of guitar No. 1 until it's at what you feel is the correct level for the mix. Is it clashing with another instrument? Does it cover up another instrument?

B) Pan the guitar to the opposite side of the instrument that it's clashing with. Is it clashing with another instrument now? Does it cover up another instrument?

C) Pan the guitar around the soundfield to see if there's a spot where you can distinctly hear it without it clashing with another instrument. Is it still clashing with another instrument? Does it cover up another instrument?

D) Using the subtractive EQ technique from Chapter 4, sweep through the mid-frequency band until you find the offending frequency, then lower it. Does the guitar still clash with the other instrument? Are they both EQ'd at the same frequency? If so, move the frequency of one higher or lower.

E) Add a bit of reverb from Reverb Two until you can just hear it. Does it sound bigger than before? Does it set it back in the mix and further away from the listener? What happens if you had more reverb?

F) Add a bit of delay to the guitar until you can just hear the effect. Does it sound bigger than before? Does it set it back in the mix and further away from the listener? What happens if you add more delay? Does it sound better than the reverb? What happens if you add both?

G) If there are other guitars, add them one by one and follow steps A through F.

Keyboards

Depending upon what role the keyboard is playing in the mix, it might be better to add it to the mix before the guitars. Generally speaking, keyboards that play long sustaining chords, like organs or strings, generally benefit from more reverb or delay than percussive sounds like piano.

Exercise Pod: Balancing The Keyboards

E13.11: Balancing The Keyboards

A) Raise the level of the keyboard until it's at what you feel is the correct level for the mix. Is it clashing with another instrument? Does it cover up another instrument?

B) Pan the keyboard to the opposite side of the instrument that it's clashing with. Is it clashing with another instrument? Does it cover up another instrument?

C) Pan the keyboard around the soundfield to see if there's a spot where it you can distinctly hear it without it clashing with another instrument? Is it still clashing with another instrument? Does it cover up another instrument?

D) Using the subtractive EQ technique from Chapter 4, search through the frequencies until you find the offending frequency, then lower it. Does the keyboard still clash with the other instrument? Are they both EQ'd at the same frequency? If so, move the frequency of one higher or lower.

E) Add a bit of reverb from Reverb Two until you can just hear the effect. Does it sound bigger than before? Does it set it back in the mix and further away from the listener? What happens if you add more reverb?

F) Add a bit of delay to the keyboard until you can just hear the effect. Does it sound bigger than before? Does it set it back in the mix and further away from the listener? What happens if you add more delay? Does it sound better than the reverb? What happens if you add both?

G) If there are other keyboards, add them one by one and follow steps A through F.

Loops

Loops are a crucial musical element these days and generally change the way you build a track, depending upon the importance of the element. If a loop is present, it's usually best to start the mix with that element, then build the mix around it. If the song is made primarily of loops, then it's important to find the combination of loops that creates the pulse of the song, then build the mix from there.

Exercise Pod: Balancing Loops

E13.12: Balancing A Loop Against The Band

A) Raise the level of the loop until it's at what you feel is the correct level for the mix. Is it clashing with another instrument? Does it cover up another instrument?

B) Pan the loop to the opposite side of the instrument that it's clashing with. Is it clashing with another instrument? Does it cover up another instrument?

C) Pan the loop around the soundfield to see if there's a spot where it you can distinctly hear it without it clashing with another instrument? Is it still clashing with another instrument? Does it cover up another instrument?

D) Using the subtractive EQ technique from Chapter 4, search through the frequencies until you find the offending frequency, then lower it. Does the keyboard still clash with the other instrument? Are they both EQ'd at the same frequency? If so, move the frequency of one higher or lower.

E) Add a bit of reverb from Reverb One until you can just hear the effect. Does it sound bigger than before? Does it set it back in the mix and further away from the listener? What happens if you add more reverb?

F) Add a bit of delay to the loop until you can just hear the effect. Does it sound bigger than before? Does it set it back in the mix and further away from the listener? What happens if you add more delay? Does it sound better than the reverb? What happens if you add both?

G) If there are other loops, add them one by one and follow steps A through F.

E13.13: Balancing A Loop-Based Song

A) Find the most important loop. Raise it so the level reads -10 dB on the mix bus meter.

B) Listen to the other loops. Which one acts as the bass, etc.? Add them into the mix as previously described.

CHAPTER 14
THE FINAL RECORDING

Now that you've made it through basic training, your ear should be more attuned to what a good recording sounds like, and your recordings should be better than ever. Like so many other things in life, recording takes practice, and the more you do it, the better you get. The more experience you gain, the more you learn what works and what doesn't in a song, and when you hear a sound in your head, you have a better idea of how to go about getting it.

Keep in mind that there are many roads to the same destination. What I've shown you in this book are some methods that definitely work, but there are others that work too. Don't be afraid to try anything, because you never know when you'll find a technique that fits your style best. Take what works and leave the rest.

Above all, have fun. You can sometimes create magic without it, but everything goes so much easier when everyone is having a good time.

You've now graduated basic training. Good luck, and go make some great mixes!

GLOSSARY

Acoustic Foam: A lightweight foam material used for acoustic control.

ADC: Analog to Digital Converter. This device converts the analog waveform into the digital form of digital 1s and 0s.

Attack: The first part of a sound. On a compressor/limiter, a control that affects how that device will respond to the attack of a sound.

Attenuation: A decrease in level.

Automation: A system that memorizes, then plays back the position of all faders, mutes, and sometimes panning and EQ on a console or in a DAW.

Aux Send: Stands for "auxiliary send," which splits the signal off so it can be routed to headphones or effects.

Bandwidth: The number of frequencies that a device will pass before the signal degrades. A human being can supposedly hear from 20Hz to 20kHz, so the bandwidth of the human ear is 20 to 20kHz.

Bi-directional: A microphone with a figure 8 pickup pattern.

Bus: A signal pathway.

Capsule: The part of a microphone that contains the primary electronic pickup element.

Cardioid: A microphone that has a heart-shaped pickup pattern.

Chorus: A type of signal processor that mixes a detuned copy with the original signal, which creates a fatter sound.

Click: A metronome feed to the headphones to help the musicians play at the right tempo.

Clip: To overload and cause distortion.

Close Miking: Placing a mic close to an instrument in order to decrease the pickup of room reflections or other sound sources.

Color: To affect the timbral qualities of a sound.

Condenser: A microphone that uses two electrically charged plates (thereby creating an electronic component known as a "condenser") as its basis of operation.

Cue Mix: The headphone mix sent to the musicians that differs from the one that the producer and engineer are listening to (see Chapter 8).

Cut: To decrease, attenuate, or make less.

DAW: A digital audio workstation. A computer with the appropriate hardware and software needed to digitize and edit audio.

Decay: The time it takes for a signal to fall below audibility.

Delay: A type of signal processor that produces distinct repeats (echoes) of a signal.

DI: Direct Injection; an impedance matching device that bypasses the use of a microphone.

Diaphragm: The element of a microphone moved by sound pressure.

Direct: To "go direct" means to bypass a microphone and connect the guitar, bass, keyboard, etc. directly into a recording device.

Direct Box: see "Direct"

Directional: A microphone that has most of its pickup pattern in one direction.

Double: To play or sing a track a second time. The inconsistencies between both tracks make the part sound bigger.

Dynamic: A dynamic microphone changes acoustic energy into electrical energy by the motion of a diaphragm through a magnetic field.

Edgy: A sound with an abundance of mid-range frequencies.

Envelope: Every sound can be broken down into a beginning (the attack), a middle (the sustain), and an end (the release). This is referred to as the "volume envelope."

EQ: Equalizer, or to adjust the equalizers (tone controls) to affect the timbral balance of a sound.

Equalizer: A tone control that can vary in sophistication from very simple to very complex (see Parametric Equalizer).

Figure 8: A microphone with a pickup pattern primarily from the front and rear.

Flam: A sound source played slightly off-time with another.

Gain Stage: Any stage or point in an audio/video signal path where the gain or level of the signal can be adjusted or amplified. Basically this means any piece of equipment the signal passes through can be considered at least one gain stage (if not many stages). Any place your signal encounters a level control is a gain stage.

Gobo: A portable wall used to isolate one sound source from another.

Groove: The pulse of the song and how the instruments dynamically breathe with it.

Ground: A switch on some audio devices (mostly guitar amps and direct boxes) used to decrease hum.

Group: When the faders of several mixer channels are linked together so they move all at the same time, they are in a group.

High End: The high-frequency part of a sound.

High-Pass Filter: An electronic device that allows the high frequencies to pass while attenuating the low frequencies. Used to eliminate low frequency artifacts like hum and rumble.

Impedance: The electronic measurement of the total electronic resistance to an audio signal.

Input Buffer: A temporary memory location that collects the bursts of digital information and sends it smoothly to the CPU in the computer.

I/O: The Input/Output of a device.

Latency: Latency is a measure of the time it takes (in milliseconds) for your audio signal to pass through your system during the recording process. This delay is caused by the time it takes for your computer to receive, understand, process, and send the signal back to your outputs.

Layer: To make a larger more complex sound picture by adding additional tracks via overdubbing.

Leakage: Acoustic spill from a sound source other than the one intended for pickup.

Leslie: A speaker cabinet, usually used with a Hammond organ, that features rotating high and low frequency speakers.

Line Level: The normal operating signal level of most professional audio gear. The output of a microphone is boosted to line level by a preamplifier.

Low End: The low frequency part of a sound.

Make-up Gain: A control on a compressor/limiter that applies additional gain to the signal. This is required since the signal is automatically decreased when the compressor is working. Make-up Gain "makes up" the gain by bringing the signal back to where it was prior to being compressed.

Modulate: The process of adding a control voltage to a signal source in order to change its character. For example, modulating a short slap delay with a .5Hz signal will produce chorusing (see Chorus).

Mute: An On/Off switch. To mute something would mean to turn it off.

Nearfield: The listening area where there is more direct than reflected sound.

Null: The point on the microphone pickup pattern where the pickup sensitivity is at its lowest.

Off-Axis: A sound source away from the primary pickup point of a microphone.

Omnidirectional: A microphone that picks up sound equally from any direction.

On-Axis: A sound source aimed at the primary pickup point of a microphone.

ORTF: Office de Radiodiffusion Television Française; a stereo miking technique developed by the Office of French Radio and Television Broadcasting using two cardioid mics angled 110° apart and spaced seven inches (17 cm) apart horizontally.

Overheads: The microphones placed over the head of a drummer used to either pick up the entire kit, or just the cymbals (see Chapters 6 and 7).

Pad: An electronic circuit that attenuates the signal (usually either 10 or 20 dB) in order to avoid overload.

Parametric Equalizer: A tone control in which the gain, frequency, and bandwidth are all variable.

Phantom Image: In a stereo system, if the signal is of equal strength in the left and right channels, the resultant sound appears to come from in between them. This is a phantom image.

Phase Shift: The process during which some frequencies (usually those below 100Hz) are slowed down ever so slightly as they pass through a device. This is usually exaggerated by excessive use of equalization and is highly undesirable.

Plate (Reverb): A method to create artificial reverberation using a large steel plate with a speaker and several transducers connected to it.

Plug-in: An add-on to a computer application that adds functionality to it. EQ, modulation, and reverb are examples of DAW plug-ins.

Polarity: A switch on a console that reverses pins 2 and 3 in an XLR connector.

Pop Filter: A piece of acoustic foam, placed either internally near the diaphragm or externally over the mic, designed to reduce plosives, or "pops."

Preamplifier: An electronic circuit that boosts the tiny output of a microphone to a level more easily used by the other electronic devices in the studio.

Predelay: A variable length of time before the onset of reverberation. Predelay is often used to separate the source from the reverberation so the source can be heard more clearly.

Presence: Accentuated upper mid-range frequencies (anywhere from 5 to 10kHz).

Proximity Effect: The inherent low frequency boost that occurs with a directional microphone as the signal source gets closer to it.

Pumping: When the level of a mix increases, then decreases noticeably. Pumping is caused by the improper setting of the attack and release times on a compressor.

Punchy: A description for a quality of sound that infers good reproduction of dynamics with a strong impact. Sometimes means emphasis in the 200Hz and 5kHz areas.

Q: Bandwidth of a filter or equalizer.

Range: On a gate or expander, a control that adjusts the amount of attenuation that will occur to the signal when the gate is closed.

Ratio: A parameter control on a compressor/limiter that determines how much compression or limiting will occur when the signal exceeds threshold.

Recall: A system that memorizes the position of all pots and switches on a console. The engineer must still physically reset the pots and switches back to their previous positions as indicated on a video monitor.

Release: The last part of a sound. On a compressor/limiter, a control that affects how that device will respond to the release of a sound.

Resonant Frequency: A particular frequency or band of frequencies that are accentuated, usually due to some extraneous acoustic, electronic, or mechanical factor.

Return: Inputs on a recording console or DAW especially dedicated for effects devices such as reverbs and delays. The Return inputs are usually not as sophisticated as normal channel inputs on a console.

Reverb: A type of signal processor that reproduces the spatial sound of an environment (i.e. the sound of a closet or locker room or inside an oil tanker).

Ribbon: A microphone that utilizes a thin aluminum ribbon as the main pickup element.

Rolloff: Usually another word for high-pass filter, although it can refer to a low-pass filter as well.

Sibilance: A rise in the frequency response in a vocal where there's an excessive amount of 5kHz, resulting in the "S" sounds being overemphasized.

Solo: A console or DAW function that automatically mutes all other channels except the one that's selected.

Soundfield: The direct listening area.

Spaced Pair: A stereo miking technique in which the microphones are placed several feet apart.

SPL: Sound Pressure Level.

Subgroup: A fader that controls the output of a number of channels (like drums) that then feeds the master fader.

Talkback: The communication link between the control room and the cue mix in the musicians' headphones allowing the producer or engineer to speak with the musicians.

Threshold: The point at which an effect takes place. On a compressor/limiter, for instance, the Threshold control adjusts the point at which compression will take place.

Timbre: Tonal color.

Transformer: An electronic component that either matches or changes the impedance. Transformers are large, heavy, and expensive but are in part responsible for the desirable sound in vintage audio gear.

Transient: An extremely short burst of sound that may be so fast that a meter on a DAW can't track it.

Trim: A control that sets the gain of a device, usually referred to on a microphone preamplifier.

Tube: Short for vacuum tube; an electronic component used as the primary amplification device in most vintage audio gear. Equipment utilizing vacuum tubes run hot, are heavy, and have a short life, but have a desirable sound.

VU Meter: A mechanical analog meter that measures the audio level, or Volume Units, of a sound.

Windscreen: A device placed over a microphone to attenuate the noise cause by wind interference.

X/Y: A stereo miking technique in which the microphone capsules are mounted as closely as possible while crossing at 90 degrees.

BIBLIOGRAPHY

The Mixing Engineer's Handbook 2nd Edition (ISBN #1598632515—Thomson Course Technology): The premier book on audio mixing techniques provides all the information needed to take your mixing skills to the next level along with advice from the world's best mixing engineers.

The Recording Engineer's Handbook 2nd Edition (159863867X—Course Technology PTR): Revealing the microphone and recording techniques used by some of the most renowned recording engineers, you'll find everything you need to know to lay down great tracks in any recording situation, in any musical genre, and in any studio.

The Audio Mastering Handbook 2nd Edition (ISBN #1598634496—Course Technology PTR): Everything you always wanted to know about mastering, from doing it yourself to using a major facility, utilizing insights from the world's top mastering engineers.

The Drum Recording Handbook with DVD (with Dennis Moody) (ISBN #1423443438—Hal Leonard): Uncovers the secret of amazing drum recordings in your recording studio even with the most inexpensive gear. It's all in the technique, and this book/DVD will show you how.

How To Make Your Band Sound Great with DVD (ISBN #1423441907—Hal Leonard): This band improvement book and DVD shows your band how to play to its fullest potential. It doesn't matter what kind of music you play, what your skill level is, or if you play covers or your own music, this book will make you tight, it will make you more dynamic, it will improve your show, and it will improve your recordings.

The Studio Musician's Handbook with DVD (with Paul ILL) (ISBN #1423463412—Hal Leonard): Everything you wanted to know about the world of the studio musician including how you become a studio musician, who hires you and how much you get paid, what kind of skills you need and what gear you must have, the proper session etiquette required to make a session run smoothly, and how to apply these skills in every type of recording session regardless if it's in your home studio or Abbey Road.

Music 3.0—A Survival Guide To Making Music In The Internet Age (ISBN #1423474015—Hal Leonard): The paradigm has shifted and everything you knew about the music business has completely changed. Who are the new players in the music business? Why are traditional record labels, television, and radio no longer factors in an artist's success? How do you market and distribute your music in the new music world—and how do you make money? This book answers these questions and more in its comprehensive look at the new music business—Music 3.0.

The Music Producer's Handbook (ISBN 978-1423474005—Hal Leonard): Reveals the inside information and secrets to becoming a music producer and producing just about any kind of project in any genre of music. Among the topics covered are the producer's responsibilities and all the elements of a typical production, including budgeting, contracts, selecting the studio and engineer, hiring session musicians, and even getting paid! The book also covers the true mechanics of production, from analyzing and fixing the format of a song, to troubleshooting a song when it just doesn't sound right, to getting the best performance and sound out of the band and vocalist.

The Musician's Video Handbook (ISBN 978-1423484448—Hal Leonard): Describes how the average musician can easily make any of the various types of videos now required by a musical artist either for promotion or final product. But just shooting a video isn't enough. The book will also demonstrate the tricks and tips used by the pros to make it look professionally done, even with inexpensive gear and not much of a budget.

Mixing And Mastering With T-Racks: The Official Guide (ISBN 978-1435457591—Course Technology PTR): T-RackS is a popular stand-alone audio mastering application that includes a suite of powerful analog-modeled, digital dynamics, and EQ processor modules that also work perfectly as plug-ins during mixing. While T-RackS is an extremely powerful tool for improving the quality of your recordings, all of that power won't do you much good if it's misused. With *Mixing and Mastering with IK Multimedia T-RackS: The Official Guide*, you can learn how to harness the potential of T-RackS and learn the tips and tricks of using T-Racks processor modules to help bring your mixes to life, then master them so they're competitive with any major label release.

The Touring Musician's Handbook (ISBN 978-1423492368—Hal Leonard): For a musician, touring is the brass ring. It's the thing that everyone dreams about from the first time they pick up an instrument. But what do you do when you finally get that chance? How do you audition? What kind of chops do you need? What equipment should you bring? How do you prepare for life on the road? Regardless of whether you're a sideman, solo performer, or member of a band, all of these questions are answered in *The Touring Musician's Handbook*. As a bonus, individual touring musician guides for guitar, bass, drums, vocals, keys, horns, and strings, as well as interviews with famous and influential touring players, are also included.

The Ultimate Guitar Tone Handbook (ISBN 978-0739075357—Alfred Music Publishing): This is the definitive book for discovering that great guitar sound and making sure it records well. It definitively outlines all the factors that make electric and acoustic guitars, and amplifiers and speaker cabinets sound the way they do, as well as the classic and modern recording and production techniques that capture great tone. *The Ultimate Guitar Tone Handbook* also features a series of interviews with expert players, technicians, recording engineers, producers, and manufacturers that gives you an inside look into the business of guitar tone. An accompanying DVD provides both an audio and visual reference point for achieving the classic sounds you hear on records.

The Studio Builder's Handbook (ISBN—978-0739077030 Alfred Music Publishing): No matter how good your recording gear is, chances are you're not getting the best possible sound because of the deficiencies of your room. While you might think that it costs thousands of dollars and the services of an acoustic designer to improve your studio, *The Studio Builder's Handbook* will strip away the mystery of what makes a great sounding studio and show how you can make a huge difference in your room for as little as $150.

You can get more info and read excerpts from each book by visiting bobbyowsinski.com.

Bobby Owsinski's Social Media Connections

Bobby's Music Production Blog: bobbyowsinski.blogspot.com

Bobby's Music Industry Blog: music3point0.blogspot.com

Bobby on Facebook: facebook.com/bobby.owsinski

Bobby on Twitter: @bobbyowsinski

Bobby on YouTube: youtube.com/polymedia

INDEX